In the beginning the Word already existed;
the Word was with God,
and the Word was God.
From the very beginning
the Word was with God.
Through him God made all things;
not one thing in all creation
was made without him.
The Word was the source of life,
and this life brought light to humanity.
The light shines in the darkness,
and the darkness has never put it out.

Chosen
Before Creation

Chosen
Before Creation

Mohammad Mihandoust

ISBN-13: 978-0-578-40911-5

Library of Congress Control Number: 2018915154

Printed in the United States of America

Typesetter: Michelle Kenny, Windsor, CO

Cover Designer & Photo Credit: Miss Bahareh Kamankesh

Table of Contents

Acknowledgements

God is the true author of this book. I thank Him for the honor of being His humble servant in sharing His message to the world.

From the bottom of my heart I would like to thank Miss Connie J. King. She put in endless hours of work typing and editing. Thank you, too, Miss Betsy Smith for her great job on the final editing. She is a very passionate and strong Christian.

Finally, I thank Miss Bahareh Kamankesh, who did all the artwork and photoshopping. She brought my vision of blessing to life for all to see and understand. God bless you all.

Preface

There is a powerful living God. He is holy, kind, and loving. There is salvation and a way to get there. It is only through Jesus Christ. He is the way. My goal for writing this book is to pass on a true message from Holy God. His desire is for you to understand His magnificent love for humanity. It is a beautiful love story.

We know a lot about God. If we pay attention we can see His fingerprints everywhere. When you look at the ocean and the mountains, the sky and the stars you can see what He has created. Look in the mirror. What do you see? You were created by God as were your precious children. He also made things we cannot see, the Spiritual Realm.

But what about Satan? What do you know about him and his role in the world? You may say, "Not much and actually I don't want to know about him." That's because you are afraid of him. Even some preachers don't know much about him. When asked, "How come you don't inform us of the Devil?" they say they don't want to give power to him by talking about him. But the fact is you cannot. God already did and when He did, He was very generous.

Before creation there was nothing but God Himself. Satan was created by God to be very attractive. God called him Lucifer. He was next to God all the time. God gave Lucifer power, but remember the highest power is God. Satan saw God's glory, and wanted to be God. He wanted to be worshipped by angels. He was trying to associate himself with God, thinking he could do the same thing and everyone would worship him. He didn't want to accept that God had created him.

One day Lucifer betrayed God because of his arrogance, ignorance, and self-importance. He even claimed he would build his throne above God's. His ego is monstrous and he has no humility.

Demons are those dark angels that thought just like Lucifer with the same evil mentality. God threw them all out of Heaven. Ever since then they have worked 24 hours a day to pull humankind away from God. They are all around us.

Satan cannot see the future, but God can. Satan cannot be in a few places at once, but God can be everywhere. I'm not trying to compare Satan to God because there is no comparison. I never had faith, the way I do now. Because of my experience, I know God can do everything. He can save everyone and forgive everyone. This is His kingdom.

> *"I am the Lord, I show mercy and kindness to anyone I choose. I will let you see my glory and hear my Holy name." Exodus 33:19, (Contemporary English Version)*

Now that we know Satan and his demons exist, we need to understand their purpose which is to destroy us and pull us away from God. This book will help you recognize their capabilities and strategies so you can be armed and ready for successful battle. Since Satan's victory over Adam and Eve, he has been at battle with God and God's people. Satan works at a personal level. He knows our weaknesses and uses them to make us commit sins.

Much of mankind doesn't understand the deep attachment we inherently have to the things that belong to this world. That is why many of us cannot find God and understand our true purpose for being on earth.

Sometimes I ask why? Why have I experienced all these incredible miracles? Why has God called me through three prophetic dreams? Why has God blessed me and demonstrated His blessings from Heaven? Why did He speak to me out loud? Why did I see the Devil and his demons in my house? Why has God allowed me to suffer so much and why my nature has changed so dramatically? What power transformed me?

When people think about Hell, they imagine fire, which most people fear. However, there is something even worse; when our spirit is tormented by the Devil. I believe no one can handle that. I have gone through Hell and it's quite painful. Some days I wish not to be alive anymore because I feel so disturbed. When I was not walking with God I did not feel any of these attacks, but eight months after my baptism the attacks started.

In the past, these evil spirits obviously were very happy with me because I was doing exactly what they wanted. However, today they hate me and for a strong reason. I love and obey God. I have no fear of Satan because God is on my side. Unfortunately, Satan has control of many people and the sad thing is that they don't even know it. He wants to keep it that way. He wants our children, our grandchildren, and us to be destroyed. But why? It comes from his disgusting nature. I pray every day that Satan and his army will go to Hell as I pray.

God wants to tell us that wake up time is running out. Soon we will leave this world and after we leave we cannot come back to clean up our mess ever again. I know that God wants us to repent and ask for forgiveness and simply walk away from Satan and his temptations.

God is all-powerful and nothing can go against Him. Therefore, if you have God on your side, you shouldn't be afraid of the Devil.

I hope my book changes many people's destinies and takes them to God, because no one wants to be with Satan. This is my journey from Islam to Christianity. I have been witness to God's miracles and Satan's mayhem. Everything I have written in this book actually happened. Each day, before I would begin to write, I'd ask God to please tell me exactly what He wanted me to write, no more, no less. Nothing in this world is that important as to use God's name for something that is not true. I have no desire to betray God in any way whatsoever. I pray that you believe my story and that you experience first-hand, miracles of your own.

God bless you.

Chapter 1

My First School and The First Dream

At the end of 2004, on a low budget and with used furniture, I opened my first barbering school in Northridge, California. The landlord said he would renovate the place with classrooms and offices. He kept his promise. After the State Board visit, they gave me permission to start. I also met a nice man who helped me with all the required basic documents I needed. He had experience as he worked at another school. He helped me a lot.

I was doing everything else myself. I was the boss, teacher, janitor, and owner. Honestly, I didn't have the experience to run a school, but I was very good at training students and cutting hair, which was the key to my success.

I couldn't work at my barbershop anymore because I wanted to run my school. My income stopped. The six employees I had went to work at the beauty shop next door. My entire clientele went with them. I felt betrayed and alone again. After 17 years I had to put my shop up for sale. The woman next door bought it. I had no choice. I couldn't handle both.

In the beginning of 2005, my student load was increasing and the school had a nice vibe. I worked very hard to train them to be professional barbers. My students needed to practice cutting hair. So I had a jeep I would park on the street with a sign behind it advertising $3.50 for haircuts. Customers waited for hours to get a cut. I was so busy I would forget to move my car back to the school. I wasn't supposed to park after 4:00 p.m., so I got many tickets. I trusted my students and let them handle money from our clients. They were honest.

One day a very polite man inquired about being a student. His name was José Luis. I enrolled him. I didn't know it at the time, but he would turn out to be very important to my future.

We had an increase in clients, so I was able to save more money for expenses. Tuition was quite low to keep the students content. There was a three-year wait to apply for financial aid for the school. I had to prove to the government I could survive by getting everyone licensed at a high percentage rate. Of course, getting money from students was hard. Some of them had no intention of paying, but most were very good about it. Some of my new students were former clients from my first barbershop. In fact, the first student to enroll had been a client and was able to pay for the entire course.

We had two types of students in the school. One group actually wanted to learn and worked hard to build their future. They paid and cooperated with everything on time and were honest, even with their time cards.

Other students though, would cheat by clocking in and out for their friends who weren't even there. This group didn't care, and created problems. They were disrespectful and wouldn't pay the cost of school. The success of the first group was on par. The second group lacked enthusiasm and aspirations.

When my first student passed the State Boards, the school was invigorated. She had already had a cosmetology license, but we didn't have enough time to train her in barbering. She had only 400 hours, and I was concerned, but she passed.

I was in the classroom teaching theory when she walked in, smiled and showed us her license. It was very exciting for us all. The students saw she had only three months training, and were encouraged about passing the Boards. My goal was to have a 100% pass rate.

I needed the school as it was all I had. I taught theory, but my English was not great. This made me anxious about being teased by students. Some did laugh. Barbering and cosmetology education was very professional and technical. At home during the evenings, I would read a line at least ten times to get the pronunciation right. I would highlight it, find it in my medical dictionary and translated it into my language so that I was able to understand and then teach it. The class included history, anatomy and physiology, professional image, coloring, sanitation, disinfection and much more. I felt like I was a medical doctor. I had to try to pronounce these words correctly. One of my students knew dialysis and said my pronunciations were good. That made me feel good and gave me confidence.

One evening, Mr. José Luis walked into my office and said he needed to speak with me. He said, "I had a dream last night about you."

9

The First Dream
(paraphrased)

I was somewhere beautiful, vivid and awesome, not here on Earth. I was standing next to a creek surrounded by gorgeous trees and nature's most exquisite surroundings. The water was clean and crystal clear. I could see the bottom rocks and algae. I was exploring and enjoying the environment. Rocks were positioned across the creek so I could leap onto them to the other side.

Walking by the creek up a hill I saw a big house. I walked around the back of the house and found a large door halfway open. I went inside, but there was nothing there, no furniture and no one.

I called out, "Hello, hello, hello." No answer. I turned around and saw a woman with long hair and a long white dress standing in front of me.

I said, "Sorry Ma'am. I didn't see you."

She said, "It's okay José Luis, but you need to go back."

I asked, "How do you know my name?"

"I know everything about you, but you must leave now."

I apologized and went outside. I was enamored with the beauty around me.

Ahead I saw a little white elephant playing in a mud pond, tossing the mud up over its back with its trunk, getting quite dirty. When the mud slid down, the elephant turned white again. The elephant repeated this again and again, always becoming pure white. This place was so fascinating. It was joyful. By the creek again, was this same woman just gazing at me.

I said, "Oh, it's you again."

She answered, "José Luis, I want you to give a message to someone."

"A message to whom?" I asked.

"Mohammad," she answered.

"Who is that?" (In my dream I didn't know any Mohammad.

"Your teacher."

I said, "Oh, yes. What is it?"

"Tell Mohammad he is going to climb a mountain and worship God soon."

That was the end of the dream. *(See Photo 1.1)*

I asked José what it meant, but he didn't know. He was a Christian, a polite, kindhearted person. Perhaps because of his kindness, God chose him to give me this message. I thanked him and returned to my work. His dream mystified me. It was on my mind and I wanted the meaning. I sensed it was good, but I didn't realize this was a call from God.

> *"16 I have other sheep that are not in this sheep pen. I must bring them together too, when they hear my voice. Then there will be one flock of sheep and one shepherd." John 10:16, (C.E.V.)*

I was studying and teaching a lot at night as the school was open from 8:00 a.m. until 9:00 p.m. It was exhausting and difficult. I was extremely attached to my students. Most of

(Photo 1.1)

them were hard workers and wanted to finish school as fast as possible in order to begin employment as professional barbers. Some of them just wanted to get the hours for their licenses.

I told them, "A license doesn't prove you're competent, so why waste your time and money?" They didn't care, paid no attention, and had no goals. I had students that needed help who couldn't pay for school, but were positive and determined, so I helped them. Some didn't pay and still didn't care.

I had a student named David, an old time barber, who had no license. He was a master barber with much experience. David was not only my student, but helped me so much working on the floor to train students.

One day a gentleman walked in. He had one hand and a hook for the other. He wanted to learn. I said to him with all due respect, he needed both hands. He insisted I give him a chance. I called David into my office to consult. He said to give him a chance. So we did.

This guy was determined, very smart, and positive. He would hold the comb with the hook and the clipper with his hand. With every motion, he changed the direction of his hook. He shaved faces the same way. We were all amazed.

After a while he became quite proficient. When he went to the State Board they, too, were surprised. He came back with his license. We were all so happy for him and everyone was inspired and enthusiastic.

At the end of the course many received their proof of training, and were on the road to changing their lives. A few even opened their own barbershops.

Running the school was becoming too much as enrollment was increasing. I needed business help, so I hired a woman who unfortunately proved to be a quite difficult person. But because I didn't have any other help or experience, I had to deal with her.

To qualify the school for financial aid, I attended government seminars which were costly and I had to travel to other states. It was stressful especially with a small budget.

As the year progressed more students started to take the boards and got their licenses, usually on the first try. Another beauty school was competing with us and started teaching barber classes. Although they had financial aid, my school had a better reputation. Almost everyone in the San Fernando Valley knew of it.

The first time I had tried for financial aid, I didn't make it. We couldn't pass the requirements of the agency that works for the government. I asked them why, but they just faxed the results. It was so disappointing. My students came to me with much sympathy and consolations.

That night as I was in the car going home I stopped at a red light. The license plate in front of me read, "Relax God is in Charge." I was instantly very calm. I had that saying printed and tacked it to my wall.

Chapter 2

Moving Closer to God

I now lived in an apartment on Ventura Boulevard. Late one night I was sitting in front of my computer listening to music with the TV behind me on mute. To my right was the kitchen with a stove light on. I was depressed and began talking to God and crying. This was the first time in my life I had cried so hard. I asked Him to bless me with many different things, whatever I could think of. In the middle of my sobbing, I heard the TV click off by itself.

I said aloud, "Oh, my God, you heard my prayer!" *(See Photo 2.1)*

I was in such disbelief that this happened. I pondered on it for a while and finally went to bed. When I woke up in the morning I remembered José Luis' dream and the TV. Was there a connection?

No one could tell me the meaning. Almost every day I thought about it. When I saw José at school I asked about the dream

(Photo 2.1)

again, and I told him how the TV turned itself off. Neither of us could figure it out.

An Iranian student, a Christian, enrolled in my school. He was a real nice guy. From the start he talked to me almost every day about Christianity and Jesus Christ, but I didn't want to hear it. He was respectful toward me and vice versa.

> *"The God who rules this world has blinded the minds of unbelievers. They cannot see the light, which is the good news about our glorious Christ, who shows what God is like." 2 Corinthians 4:4, (C.E.V.)*

He stayed in my school for one and a half years and he tried hard to help me find Christ. He even gave me a Bible, which I never read. He shared the good news of the gospel, but to make someone believe is God's work alone. God knows who will answer and who will not. I believe God knocks on everyone's door, but many don't open it to Him. He is willing, but we are not.

"Many are invited, but only a few are chosen." Matthew 22:14, (C.E.V.)

We had re-applied for financial aid. When the report was due the entire school was in the office awaiting the results. When the fax came through saying we got the financial aid we were all elated. They took a picture of me holding the document. I was so proud. It was such an honor to have the aid, having worked so hard to get it.

Other schools heard that my school was thriving. Things were looking up. Tuition was now guaranteed and I could improve the entire school and move to a better location. We enrolled many needy students. Those that couldn't even speak English and even people who had spent time in prison got their licenses. They were becoming prosperous.

Barbershops popped up all over the valley because of our graduates. Around this time my mother passed away. I felt my happiness drain from my spirit. The students were my family now, as my birth family was far away. But every week another student would graduate and leave. I felt such a loss over and over.

The State Board people knew my school well. They could tell my students by their style of cutting hair. I could make anyone a professional barber in one and a half years, which is rare. I used to tell my students to give me a year and I would give them a future, and it was true. I was finally able to hire an instructor to work for me teaching theory. I was relieved just to be training on the floor. But this was always interesting.

My master barber, David got his license and left school, so I was all alone again. One day I saw him and asked him to work at my school. He agreed and there we were again. After a short time, he began complaining about his health. In a few months it was discovered he had liver cancer and he passed away. Such a tragedy. My students and I went to the funeral. It was a very sad day.

The class was close to graduation now, and new students were coming in. I started to provide food for them on Fridays as I knew some were unable to buy much food. I did this for one year. Our reputation was great and we had many clients. Our haircuts were professional and the customers were happy. Parking was becoming a problem though because we took over the lot. Both the restaurant next door and our landlord weren't happy with us.

José Luis was ending his time here also and I was sad as we had a wonderful bond. He was a good guy and had brought me the message. I gave him his diploma and he simply walked away. He said he couldn't even look at me because of his tears, but he did call me when he received his license, and soon after, he opened his own barbershop. I went to visit him and I was so proud of him. A few years after that he moved out of state to live with his daughter. I still miss him.

New students coming in were less serious as they didn't have to pay fees. It was difficult working with some of them. I felt the vibe of my school changing. As more and more students arrived the parking lot was becoming a larger problem. An agent from the Board came by to visit my school. She commented on our great success and appreciated what we were doing for the area. With all the new barbershops popping up, it was benefiting the Board and the community. There were Iranians in town who needed help so I advertised in the Iranian newspaper. My ad ran for a long time and many Iranians came into my school.

At this point, it was getting closer for the five-year lease option renewal. The landlord's manager told me not to worry, but the deadline passed and the landlord did not keep his promise. I was given one month to move. It was overwhelming. I had no idea where I was going to move to with all these students in tow. The State Board wouldn't be pleased with this. The landlord's manager apologized to me, but told me I must leave. My attorney suggested that I try to get an extension from the landlord for more time which I was granted. I spent a lot of money on the attorney fees.

I began searching for a new location for the school. I found a quite large space in a busy center. They wanted first and last month's rent and collateral, which was my house. That process alone took two months. Then there was the remodeling. Soon the city approved our new business and we were able to move.

We did a lot of costly renovations. The new place was beautiful. I couldn't believe it was mine. We had an open house to celebrate and so many friends and former students came. We were finally established again and open for business.

Yet Another School

After one year I decided to start a second school which would include cosmetology and barbering. I found a great place in Encino near an Iranian community. And again much money was spent on renovations. I was going forward without thinking I would fall because I was confident. I now had over 200 students.

We had a grand opening celebration at the new school with Mariachis, food, and a lot of people. We were all quite excited. The teaching staff would be divided between the schools. I had to go back to teaching and would work at the smaller Encino school teaching cosmetology.

Chapter 3

More Dreams

One morning, on an extremely busy school day, Shabnam, my friend who had immigrated from Morocco called telling me her mother had contacted her three times that morning saying she had a dream about me the night before. Though her mother lived in Morocco she had seen a picture of me. Curious, but wanting to give her my full attention, I asked her tell me when I got home.

The Second Dream
(paraphrased)

My mother said we three were walking in a barren desert. In front of us was a huge mountain. You started walking faster and faster to the mountain by yourself. You were going up the mountain. It looked extremely difficult, but you climbed easily. At the top you stood, face up to the sky, raised your arms, and said something in a different language.

That was the end of the dream. *(See Photo 3.1)*

(Photo 3.1)

I was stunned and asked, "What does this mean? A few years ago someone else had a dream about me that I was going to a mountain to worship God and now your mother has a similar dream. How bizarre." Now I started to take the dreams seriously. This person was a Muslim.

I had rented three billboards, one in Encino, Van Nuys and one on Fallbrook Avenue. School was getting very crowded. More and more students passed their Boards. We now had 27 employees. Our overhead alone was $120,000 monthly, but anything extra went to school expenses.

My Iranian students were going to the boards now and passing at 100% even though English was their second language. This was better than most schools. We were determined to be number one.

But I began to get lawsuits even from my Iranian students. I met with an attorney. He wanted me to put my credit card number on file so he could charge me for consecutive lawsuits. I was scared and realized I could actually fail at any time.

One of my hard working students, Jasmine, who was of the Bahá'í faith, said she wanted to instruct at my school. She proved herself to me, got both licenses, and became an excellent, enthusiastic instructor. She made me so proud and became like a sister.

One morning she came to my office to talk to me. I was curious. She said she had a dream about me the previous night. A strange feeling came over me.

The Third Dream
(paraphrased)

You had a house next to a mountain. You were cooking in the kitchen. I walked in to say, Hello and to see what was going on.

 You said, "I'm going to the mountain to do something."

I responded, "Oh, my grandpa is up there."

You asked, "Is he dead?" and I said he was.

We both went outside and you started walking toward the mountain while I waited. Then you began climbing. It looked like a very difficult climb, but you did it effortlessly, higher and higher to the top. You became small, and then disappeared. I waited for some time before I saw you coming down. When you got to me, you had a bunch of grapes on your left shoulder and you gave me a handful.

27

That was the end of the third dream. *(See Photo 3.2)*

(Photo 3.2)

I asked her what she thought it meant and told her about the first two dreams. It was a mystery to both of us. At this point I knew something important was going to happen.

I had to continue with my business and do my best for the school. I hired a young advertising agent named Rose, to be admissions counselor because she spoke Farsi. We turned into good friends and soon started dating. I met her family and we became even more involved. Everyone knew she was like my 'fiancé'. We began living together while we were also working together.

One day I noticed I had a medical issue. I went to the doctor and he referred me to a urologist. After some testing he told me I had testicular cancer. My head was hot and confused.

I asked him, "Am I going to die?" He said I wasn't, but further testing needed to be done to see if the cancer was anywhere else. Shocked and distraught, I headed home. I told no one, but Rose.

A week later, at school, an Iranian woman, very respectfully, asked me how I was.

I said, "I'm fine."

Then she asked again with conviction, "No, how do you feel?"

I told her, "I'm fine. Why?"

She said, "Are you sure you're fine?"

That's when she told me she had a dream about me the night before.

The Fourth Dream
(paraphrased)

There was a room with many people all praying to God. A lady was in the middle of the room. You were sitting on your knees and holding her hand, crying loud saying, "Help me, help me, help me."

That was the end of the dream.

I told her I'd been diagnosed with testicular cancer in both testicles. She started crying and said that whatever was wrong, I would be okay. I would be fine. Though, relieved, I was still afraid.

I continued with my medical tests. After they were all done the doctor said he must operate as soon as possible to remove the testicle with the biggest lesion. The other was left as the lesion was very small. I spent one night in the hospital and then stayed home for a few days to recover.

The doctor called and gave me the pathology results. Amazingly, the cancerous tumor tested benign. This happens in only 3% of all cases. He said I wouldn't need any chemo or radiation and to see him in one year. I was so relieved. Now I could live and work again without worry.

The year passed quickly and soon it was time for another check-up. Sadly, the tumor in the other testicle became larger, which had to be removed. It meant taking testosterone for the rest of my life. But the worst thing was I could have no more kids.

I was sad, and told Rose that she was young and because of my problem, I wanted to release her so she could find someone right for her. I didn't want her to be in this predicament with me. But she refused to leave me, for which I was grateful.

Chapter 4

Devastation

During this time the government wouldn't give student loans without a high school diploma or a GED, so the number of students dropped dramatically. Enrollment dropped from 27 new students per month to four or five. It became extremely difficult to pay the bills. Everything was going wrong. Then, due to massive changes in government funding, we could go on no longer. I had enough money to survive one more month. Personnel wrote a check to everyone but me. All my employees left except for a few. Obviously, the school was shutting down.

We were all upset. The students were mad at the government. Life went from my students in their nice clean black and white uniforms lining up at the door, learning and having fun, to a complete black out. There was nothing but darkness at my school and in my heart. It was so demoralizing to me that I have never gone back to that building.

After my surgery, but I didn't want to live any longer. I had no idea how to go forward or deal with all of this. No money, numerous lawsuits in my mailbox daily, and I had two liens on my house for over $2,000,000 from two different landlords. I also filed for bankruptcy to stop the lawsuits from coming to my house. My credit went from good to bad. Plus, I was having a lot of medical procedures.

My one constant was Rose. I asked her to marry me. I wanted her to stay by my side forever. Since she was of the Bahá'í faith and I was Muslim we had a small wedding at a mosque and a little celebration. We were now husband and wife and I was so happy. But I still had a deep emptiness within me. I was so disturbed by everything that I rejected all religions and asked my wife to give both the Holy Bible and the Koran away. I was so angry with God. How could He let this happen to me?

We needed an income so I opened a barbershop in Westlake under Rose's name. Jasmine, my former employee who had the third dream, wanted to work with me again. I hired her. Rose worked there as well. I built the shop from the ground up again clientele-wise. After a year Rose and I had a disagreement and because the shop was in her name she told me to leave. She actually called the police and forced me out. We separated at that point. Now I lived alone.

I had saved phone numbers of former clients and when I found a barber job close-by, I started to reestablish my business.

At my new job the owner was an angel. I loved her more than my own sister. She treated me well. The other employees were also sweet. Financially, times were tough. I didn't even have enough for my mortgage. I had to be careful with money as most of it was gone now. I would buy one 50-cent bagel for lunch. I started to get to know the employees in my new place, but had so much hatred and anger in my heart I didn't want to talk to anyone. I was upset a lot.

Every morning, on my way to work, I would see this big, tall cross on a church. One day I decided to go into the church and speak to God. I wanted to ask Him why this was all happening to me. I had been wronged by so many.

It's difficult to explain how I felt when I entered the sanctuary. I was crying like a baby. I prayed for understanding and guidance. I felt so abandoned and just wanted to die. When I left I felt exhausted, but a little better.

Almost everyone in the new shop was a Christian. They invited me to go to church with them. The sermon was on forgiveness. As soon as the pastor told us to forgive, I broke down in tears. My heart was slowly softening. Church was giving me a good feeling, but I never thought I'd become a Christian.

I started Bible study and met a lot of nice people, some of whom became my clients and good friends. I was invited to a Christmas party. There I met a beautiful man named Rex. He was the pastor of a small church. He, too, became one of my clients. Eventually, I told him about the dreams. He realized God was moving in my life, but didn't know what it all meant. I began attending his church where I met even more people. I was feeling much happier now, more contented.

After several months, however, I got an unexpected phone call from Rose. She wanted me to come back to the shop because she needed me. I figured things could get better financially. We met at a restaurant. I told her I would come back, but I need to talk to an attorney and have an agreement that we would own the shop equally.

She agreed and we signed the papers. It made me feel more comfortable and secure. I gave two weeks' notice to my boss who was quite distraught to be losing a good friend and brother. Everyone in that shop cared for me and I loved them. The last day I was there, they had a good-bye party for me. I went back to work at my newly half-owned shop. Rose noticed I seemed calmer at work and wondered why.

Chapter 5

The Baptism

One Saturday night after service, I suddenly had the yearning to go to Christ and become Christian. I asked Pastor Rex to baptize me.

He said, "What?"

I said, "Baptize me!"

He asked if I was serious. He was so excited to baptize a Muslim. I told him I wanted to be baptized in the ocean. He thought that was amazing and asked when. In a few days it was all arranged; May 2, 2015, at Zuma Beach, Tower #9, at 9:00 a.m. It was announced in church and everyone was thrilled. Looking forward to the baptism, I tried to understand the dreams.

> "Your glorious power will be seen on the day you begin to rule.
> You will wear the sacred robes and shine like the morning sun
> in all of your strength." Psalms 110:3, (C.E.V.)

(See Photo 5.1)

(Photo 5.1)

Even though Rose had a place of her own, she started to live at my house off and on. That made me happy. Rose decided to attend my Baptism which was nice. One week passed and Saturday morning at 8:00 a.m. we started driving to Zuma Beach. From Pacific Coast Highway, I could see the ocean, so immense, powerful and awesome. I still didn't understand what was to happen. I parked my car at Tower #9. Many people were waiting for me. I greeted everyone and we all held hands and prayed. Pastor Rex asked me if I was ready.

I said, "Yes, I am."

So my best Christian friend Pastor Rex and I started to walk into the ocean. The sky was so blue and the ocean so powerful. I'm going under water to be baptized, I thought.

Pastor asked, "Do you believe in Jesus Christ, the Son of God, who died on the cross and rose again?"

I answered, "Yes."

Then he said, "I baptize you in the name of the Father, the Son, and the Holy Spirit."

He put me under the water. I didn't realize then that I died that day and would be reborn to a new life.

Afterward everyone congratulated me. We prayed and broke bread. I felt cleansed and loved. This act was God's will. God accepted me at that very moment. *(See Photo 5.2)*

(Photo 5.2)

Chapter 6

God's Voice

I was thinking of Him more than ever now. I lived in a nice quiet neighborhood with beautiful mature trees and a lot of wildlife. Crickets were always chirping. Every night I would take walks and talk to God. In the past, if I would see someone talking to themselves I'd wonder why, but I was talking to God not myself. Some of my neighbors saw me and may have believed it was strange.

I looked forward to nighttime to walk and talk with God. I had a feeling He was listening closely to me. I talked about my life and He would listen. My mind was opening wider and wider. He was communicating with me. I could hear Him.

One night I felt Him telling me that Christianity is all about helping others. This I understood clearly. I had a holy, beautiful feeling. Early on, I heard that I was not to look at any other women, but my wife. I realized these were holy desires of God. When I went home I told Rose I received these messages. She listened politely, but I don't think she believed me. I knew now, the meaning of those dreams – my spiritual journey had begun.

My wife gifted me with a beautiful a cross and chain. Sometime later, I also bought a cross necklace of crucifix nails with a leather cord. I hung it on my rear-view mirror in my car so I could be reminded that He gave me the longing and power to obey.

Pastor Rex gave me a Bible. He wrote some encouraging words and signed it. I told him I didn't know anything about the Bible, even how to read it. I didn't even understand how to get to Heaven as a Christian. I had so much to learn. I put it on top of the fireplace under a big cross I had purchased.

I felt myself changing. One day I was sitting in the living room with Rose listening to music and talking. Suddenly, the cross on the wall drew my attention.

The cross was telling me, "I am your God." I didn't mention it. How could I explain this to her? My love for God was increasing. I could hardly wait for my walk so I could talk with Him.

Five days after my baptism, as I was taking my evening walk, I felt I was going to receive a message. Then the most amazing, holiest thing happened. I heard the voice of a man say out loud in Farsi, "Now I'm going to bring you two to three levels higher in your holiness, but you will have to be more responsible." The voice was like that of a 50-year-old man, very calm, smooth, and clear. I knew instantly it was God. When he finished, I repeated the message to myself. This was not a small voice and not my imagination. It was the voice of

God. I remembered all the dreams and it finally made sense. God was calling me.

After all these years, the predictions in the dreams were coming true. God didn't forget His promise that I would be closer to Him. He had a plan for me. It was to make me holy. My mind was spinning. The Creator of the universe spoke to me in a real voice. My ears heard His voice. Nothing can change that. *(See Photo 6.1)*

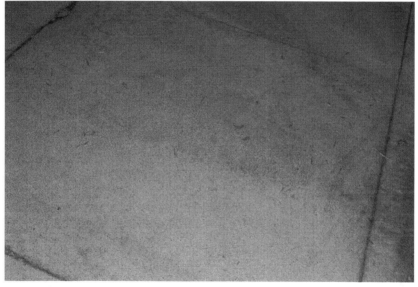

(Photo 6.1)

I wondered what two to three levels holier meant. I sensed it was up to me how far I would go with Him. God knows what He's doing. I have to rise to the level God desires. However, I still don't know the level I am at. It's all up to Him. Who knows His mind?

I wanted to tell everyone that God spoke to me; the same God who spoke to Abraham, Moses, and the angels. I was honored and humbled. Then I realized I should be more discreet for reasons that people may not believe or may think I have a mental issue. I was gradually getting to know more and more of God's wishes for my life. The next day when I woke up, I realized this experience would alter my entire life, but I was still confused.

Chapter 7

Miracle

At this point I must mention in the past I wouldn't mind going out with any woman. I didn't care, like many men. This held no moral application for me. A few days after I heard God's voice, a strange thing happened. I went home after work, took a shower and was sitting on the couch watching TV. There was a commercial of a beautiful woman in her under garments. I looked away abruptly, but it wasn't me turning my head.

I said, "Oh, my God, what is happening?" I instantly knew I couldn't look at those images anymore. I waited for 15 seconds. My head was still turned. I put my hand in front of the TV to make sure the image was gone. I slowly turned my face back to look through the cracks of my fingers. The ad was gone. From then on I had no wish to "check women out" or associate with them like before. *(See Photos 7.1 & 7.2)*

God's proclamation to make me holier was working within me. My life would never be the same. I wasn't afraid, just bewildered. Was it because of my baptism? I told Pastor Rex

(Photo 7.1)

(Photo 7.12)

about it. He is such a nice man and listened, but I think he found it hard to believe. I knew God was inside me, teaching me, working in me, and making me purer every day.

Peter said, *"Turn back to God! Be baptized in the name of Jesus Christ, so that your sins will be forgiven. Then you will be given the Holy Spirit." Acts 2:38, (C.E.V.)*

I realized I had stopped all foul language. I had no wish to look at women in a lustful way and couldn't associate with them anymore like before. I wondered what kind of power this was; all these new spiritual experiences. Most of all I knew I loved God more and more every day. How can I describe this love? My love of God is so profound that I have a strong yearning to obey Him. This makes it easy to not sin.

I talk to Him daily and tell Him how much I love Him. When I pray I forget my worldly problems and feel full of joy. Sometimes I ask myself where this feeling comes from. Is it real? When I read the Holy Bible, I see that His wish is for us to love Him. We were created to love God. He wants us to be close to Him. When He created Adam and Eve, He enjoyed their relationship. In the evening He walked with them in the Garden. How amazing. He loved them so much, but they didn't understand His passion. So when Satan tempted them, they disobeyed God. That was the beginning of sin and shame.

I told God, "I love you so much, and know that you want me to love you even more. I want to be in your world, pay attention to and obey only you." I am in love with my Creator and only want to dwell on Him. Sharing my spiritual journey with Pastor Rex brings us both joy.

"God is love. If we keep on loving others, we will stay one in our hearts with God, and he will stay one with us." 1 John 4:16, (C.E.V.)

"We love him because he first loved us." 1 John 4:19, (C.E.V.)

One night I asked God if He was listening. I felt Him say, "Of course, I'm here."

This was a new experience for me. God was actually waiting for me to go to Him, and I realized that He is waiting for everyone. Even after 58 years of separation from God I ask and He says, "Of course." He wants me to talk to Him. I believe He enjoys our conversations. He knows I'm telling Him the truth from my heart because He already knows what's in my heart. God is waiting for all people to ask for forgiveness. He will accept everyone.

In Heaven, the house of God must be an incredible place with His angels and vast kingdom. I asked God if it was true that someday I will come to live with Him. This was important and I was really wondering about its validity. My pastor told me that anyone who believes in Jesus Christ is invited into Heaven. It was so awesome to hear this.

Even though I was a changed man, I would occasionally look at a pretty woman. Old habits are hard to change. I was in my shop sitting in one of the barber chairs. Suddenly, a voice came to me and said, "You're still looking?"

I stood up immediately, surprised to hear God speaking to me. I knew what He was trying to tell me. When I told Rose she said it was my imagination. After that day I didn't say anything more about such things.

We are all sinners by nature. So backsliding will always be a challenge. Our Heavenly Father asks us to make a choice;

be with Him or with Satan. I'm not saying it's easy to choose God, but He will give you the strength to walk away from the desires of the flesh. If you are sincere, He will help you.

Yet, when I talk to some Christians, they think that lust is okay. I don't understand. Do they have the same Holy Spirit I have? My God tells me it's not okay. What is the truth here? God even turned my face to show me how determined He was. Why should I listen to people? No, I will obey my Lord.

God saw my willingness. He could see my eyes were cleaner. Soon I didn't even want to look at any woman like that again. I wondered how this was possible. Doesn't every man see a woman as something to be craved? Wasn't this natural? But for me, this urge had been transformed.

Someone asked me why I don't look at women anymore.

He said, "Women are beautiful and God's creation, so God gave us this desire."

I replied, "She is only for her husband to look at, no one else."

In other words, the desire is only right within the bounds of proper, holy marriage. I'm so grateful to be free of this. I can't look at women the wrong way anymore. God exchanged my lustfulness for what He desires.

Human beings cannot transform themselves, it's impossible. God is the only one who can do that. Once we are His, He gives us the opportunity and help to change. If we willingly cooperate with Him, He will come and live within us and start making us holy.

So what happened after the baptism? God is against sin. Now I, too, am against sin. This is supernatural. The true holy person is one who walks with Jesus Christ. I could not save myself from Hell. It is only from Christ's sacrifice on the cross that opened Heaven's gates for us. He paid for our sins.

I was invited to Christianity before all of this, but I didn't understand it. The reason I was baptized was because God called me and gave me the desire. He showed me a higher path, and all these things happened only by the help of the Holy Spirit.

Chapter 8

Miracles From Heaven

I had received some news that was unpleasant and made me depressed. A few days after that, on November 4th 2015, during my evening walk and talk to God. I was complaining to God, "When I was a kid and when I was playing with other kids if someone would bite me, I'd go home and talk to my father. He would hold me and talk to me and make me feel good. Now I have no one. They are all gone. I have no one but you God. I need you to help me."

My words hadn't even finished when I heard a noise and felt something hit my chest. This was to become the most beautiful night in my life. I looked at the sky and saw not only stars, but beautiful, glistening balls that appeared to be made of crystals. The first ball swooped down and impacted my chest.

Stunned, I said, "What is that?"

I can't explain it, but immediately I knew what it was.

I said, "Oh, it's a blessing." Then I said, "And there is one more blessing behind it. It's coming toward me."

I knew I was in the middle of something extremely pure and powerful. The balls of crystals came down from the sky, one after another, as from an escalator and I was the target. Another one hit me. I could see there were many huge balls coming down from the sky, all in a row, quite organized. In sync they, too, impacted the center of my chest.

I was shocked and thought, *What is happening here? Where are these coming from?* My eyes started to travel upward and at one point stopped.

"Oh, my God, I know this is Heaven."

I couldn't see into Heaven, but I knew these blessings had been waiting to be released to me for a while. I could comprehend more than with just my mind's eye alone. For some reason I knew this was fact.

The gate to Heaven was open. But the angels weren't throwing the blessings, it was God Himself. At one end was God in Heaven and at the other end was me on earth with the blessings between us. He was tossing them to me one after another about every three seconds, smoothly, evenly, at the same speed and distance. Every ball was full of a blessing. One was larger than the rest and held a lot of blessings. It had a different motion. It was going from left and right, like a heavy truck traveling downhill and losing control because of a heavy load.

God told me, "Look at this one, Mohammad. It contains a lot." I somehow knew it.

As they hit me the blessings were being absorbed inside of me. They were now mine. In the beginning the balls were huge and loud and the impact was strong. But by the end they were smaller, quieter, and the impact softer. The entire holy show was about 45 seconds. I could understand it now. God gave me even the smallest blessings, the ones I'd never expected. *(See Photo 8.1)*

Now the sky was quiet again. I stood bewildered. In less than a minute, God gave me a vision to see His spiritual world. I put both hands on my chest as I stood there by myself.

Everything was perfectly staged for this holy show. It was the most profound experience of my life. There is a verse in the book of Malachi about windows of Heaven. That night God actually demonstrated that verse for me.

As I started walking again my hands were still on my chest. I had seen Heaven! I wondered who would believe me. Dazed and amazed I walked silently for another half an hour.

Then, in my mind, I heard a voice ask me if I knew what had just happened. Suddenly, a veil opened in the sky and I saw myself in space. I sensed an immense treasure within me. Not a treasure one could achieve. It is only a gift from God.

For some reason I looked at my clothes, my skin, and my hands and thought, *How could it be that someone like me could become so wealthy?* That wealth wasn't for here on Earth, but for my spiritual future. Then the vision disappeared and I walked again wondering what was happening to me. *(See Photos 8.2 & 8.3)*

(Photo 8.1)

(Photo 8.2)

(Photo 8.3)

I recalled the night the TV had turned off by itself. I had been crying and asking God for blessings. Now I realized God was in the room with me and heard my cries. Tonight it was clear to me He answered my prayers saying, "I hear you and I will bless you. I hear your prayers and I keep them in Heaven. I gave blessings to you tonight. I made you understand how wealthy with blessings you are."

I walked a little longer, then went to the market to buy three bouquets for God the Father, God the Son, and one for the Holy Spirit. I took a picture of them as a remembrance. It was difficult to sleep that night I was so awe struck.

Sometime later I read the story about King Solomon. When he became a ruler, God asked him in his dream what he would like to be given?

He replied, "I'm a young King I don't know how to deal with these people, but I want to be a great King like my father, so I need wisdom."

God told him, "I will give it to you, but you didn't ask me for wealth or to defeat your enemies and long life, but I will give you these also."

I received blessings I hadn't asked for nor expected, but I know He gave them to me that night. Even in God's eyes I am wealthy. It was the most beautiful, romantic night of my life. *(See Photo 8.4)*

God has all knowledge, power, love, and extreme generosity. He is kind, and in His heart is mercy and He loves us. I wish I had known this God sooner. I would have shared His love with my family. My mom, dad, grandma, and my sisters could

(Photo 8.4)

have been baptized. My hope is one day soon all my family will be baptized. I can say with full confidence that God has the highest wisdom and love for humanity. Why would I not want a relationship with Him? He will give me everything I need.

Now I truly live in a spiritual world and my life isn't mine anymore. I know many people don't know the world of holiness because they've never been there and don't want to go. I was one of them. I had the same sinful cravings in the past and I thought it was fun. However, when God works with a person He will exchange that person's evil lusting for the flesh for His desire to make you righteous. When you receive this righteousness you will realize how bad life has actually been.

My life goal is to never sin again. God is extremely kind to me and expects nothing from me but to be clean, holy, and obey Him. This isn't a lot to ask. I find it easy because sin is repulsive now. It gives me joy to please Him. If you ask God to work in you, and you cooperate and obey, you will soon feel the same joy.

Chapter 9

The Challenge and The Word

I owned a condo in Iran where my sister was living. Due to financial reasons I had to sell it. An Iranian attorney friend of mine who lived there handled the deal. Unfortunately, he cheated me by keeping most of my money. I was quite distraught to say the least. For the rest of the day, after I heard the bad news, anger ruled my heart.

When I left the barbershop and got into my car, I noticed that the cross I have hanging on my rear-view mirror had moved from the front of the mirror to the back. It couldn't do that by itself. I was shocked and nervous, but sensed the cross was telling me not to worry about what had happened with my attorney. My mind just knew it was God telling me, "I am aware of your situation." *(See Photos 9.1 & 9.2)*

(Photo 9.1)

I spent many nights by myself because my wife lived in her own place as well as with me. I told her I needed her and wanted her to be with me. I wasn't her boyfriend, I was her

(Photo 9.2)

husband. In the beginning she would come over frequently, but then not as much.

However, she wanted to leave it that way. We went to church a few times, but even though she saw me changing, she still didn't understand.

One night, I asked her, "Do you wish to be divorced?"

She answered, "Amen." I felt sad and dismayed.

However, as we never were legally married with a license, I asked God for permission to divorce her. I know He understood the situation. So I released her. She didn't mind.

> *"If your husband or wife isn't a follower of the Lord and decides to divorce you, then you should agree to it. You are no longer bound to that person. After all, God chose you and wants you to live at peace." 1 Corinthians 7:15, (C.E.V.)*

After that night I wouldn't look at her face anymore. This created a huge distance between us. It was uncomfortable and awkward at the shop. Now I was by myself and very lonely.

I needed a break so I went to Big Bear Lake, a mountain getaway a couple hours from my home. The scenery and solitude refreshed me. I stayed there for two days and then returned home.

Some time went by and God kept purifying me daily. I felt holier now compared to my past. I didn't want to know the old me anymore. The old me had no holiness in his character or behavior. When I was baptized that former person died under the water and I was reborn. I knew at that moment something profound had occurred. However, the levels still mystified me.

I asked God, "How much more holier do I have to be? You told me two to three levels higher. Where am I now? Am I still on the first level? If so, how powerful are the second and third levels? I believe it's up to me how far I want to go with you. God, I can't understand how far the third level is because I feel the distance between each level is huge. How holy can I get?"

I couldn't comprehend it. I just knew the third level was vast and deep. Only with God's help can a person get there. How holy the angels must be. How holy is God himself!

That's why the Scriptures say, *"I am the holy God, and you must be holy too." 1 Peter 1:16, (C.E.V.)*

Now I understand it doesn't come with practice. It's a gift from God, but a gift you must nevertheless work on. I told you before it's not easy to walk with God. We are still human. Unfortunately, the closer we become to God the more Satan attacks.

I know my experiences are unusual. Sometimes I ask, "Why me?" I don't know the answer. I just know I must obey His commands. "No means no" and there are no shortcuts.

Chapter 10

Satan's Visit

This chapter is very painful for me because I am writing about someone who is the #1 enemy of our God and the enemy of all humanity, Satan. But God wants me to write this book for others to understand.

At this point I must tell you, that anytime God allows me to have a vision or witness a miracle He also gives me the wisdom to understand it in great detail.

I am going to tell you about the most fearful night of my life. It's about an entity that is very real and truly exists. However, perhaps many of you don't want to hear or believe it. But you must know it, and realize the darkness of Satan's intentions.

I had visitation from the most powerful of unclean spirits. It was a visitation from Satan himself, and his demons in my very own house. He is the one who taught Adam and Eve how to disobey God and the one who wants to keep you in darkness and away from God until you die. He is the one who wants to BE God.

I live in a beautiful, quiet neighborhood, close to some hills. After having been to Big Bear Lake for a couple of days, upon returning home around 9:00 p.m. on Tuesday, February 2, 2016, I turned on the TV. I was standing there watching a sermon. Everything was quiet, when all of a sudden I heard hundreds of people stampeding toward my house. I was terrified and was just waiting for them to break in to come get me.

It seemed they were out planning the perfect moment to attack. Then, all of a sudden, the noise stopped. Immediately after this, I heard what sounded like a fast and furious wind in my kitchen. I saw a very dark cloud hovering at the ceiling.

I knew instantly it was a powerful unclean spirit, the highest possible rank of evil. I could clearly sense that it didn't like me, in fact it hated me. It had come for one reason and one reason only, to destroy me.

Yes, it was Satan himself. He appeared to me in the form of a dark cloud. He didn't have eyes, but I felt he was looking at me, staring. I was looking back at him with tremendous fear. I was so terrified I didn't want to look anymore so I turned away and started walking toward my keys. I grabbed them and walked out. I shut the door wondering what was happening. *(See Photo 10.1)*

Walking down my dark street, feeling extremely fearful, I wasn't able to accept nor understand the fact that I had actually seen the Devil. I did not want to go home anymore, but I had no other choice, so after about an hour I returned home.

(Photo 10.1)

With great fear, I slowly opened the door and looked into the kitchen. He was gone.

Why does he want to harm me? It is because I know Christ and I am saved. Satan wants me to be destroyed. The next day I was thinking about what had happened, and how scared I was. I needed to talk to someone, but whom? Some of the people I tried to explain this to didn't believe me, and others clearly didn't want to talk about it. So I kept it to myself.

For the next few days, I could hear someone in my mind cursing at me and disrespecting God in both Farsi and English.

That Saturday night I went to church and spoke to Pastor Rex about what had happened. He listened closely and said an unclean spirit was attacking me and he would pray for me. Nothing happened for a week.

Then one Monday morning I woke up, took a shower and went in the kitchen. Suddenly, I smelled gas. I looked at the stove. The knob was on but no flame. I was shaken. I knew right away who had done it and I realized at that moment they were trying to kill me. Extreme fear came over me. *(See Photos 10.2 & 10.3)*

I didn't have to work that day so I decided to drive to Malibu and get away from the house for a while. During the drive terrifying thoughts flooded my mind like I might die soon, what was going to happen to me, who would believe all these things? I finally arrived in Malibu village and parked my car, but was still thinking about all these things. Suddenly, I looked at my rear-view mirror and noticed the cross had moved position to the top of the end of the bar, just like

(Photo 10.2)

(Photo 10.2)

the first time with my attorney. I knew what it meant. The cross was telling me, "Don't worry I know what is happening. Nothing is going to happen to you."

I understood that message correctly. But I was still very frightened. I started shaking. *(See Photos 10.4 & 10.5)*

Why had I become so important that the Devil himself would

(Photo 10.4)   *(Photo 10.5)*

want to kill me? I remembered the night of the blessings and my spiritual journey. Then I knew. I had turned toward God and away from Satan. At this point I knew there was a spiritual war going on between good and evil.

I called Pastor Rex and told him about the gas stove incident. He didn't know what to say. He was puzzled as to why all these things were occurring. I feared he didn't believe me and if not, then who do I talk to about this? The evil ones can intimidate you wildly. Something in my mind was still cursing me. I was full of fear. I needed help. The pastor said he would pray again for the unclean spirit to leave me, but it didn't.

That night I heard footsteps, which told me there were demons attacking my house. Whenever they enter, it seems like they are searching around to become familiar with it.

When in Hawaii, before my wife left, I bought a little plaque that read, "Relax". I put it on the windowsill of my guest bathroom.

Plaque on the Floor

One day, when I came home from work, I went to use that bathroom and the plaque was on the floor. At that time my daughter was visiting me for a few days. I asked her if she had dropped it. She told me she didn't even know it was there. She had heard something fall, but didn't go to see what it was. So as to not scare her I said nothing. Satan was telling me I wouldn't be able to relax anymore. For over two years now I've been harassed by him. *(See Photos 10.6 & 10.7)*

I can feel the demons' horrible capacity for evil. One night while in bed, I felt something go through me that was like an overwhelmingly strong craving for sex. I laid there waiting to see what was next. It wasn't scary at all. In fact, that moment was extremely pleasant. I was thinking, "Who is this? Why are they doing this to me?"

My pastor thought it was the Holy Spirit telling me I needed to get married. I felt reassured and was convinced it was God's doing. This feeling was occurring almost daily now. As I was going to work and on the freeway, the same urge came over

(Photo 10.6)

(Photo 10.7)

me. For several seconds I had an extreme craving to be with a woman. It was so strange.

Another time in Big Bear I was taking a walk and felt it again. I went into my cabin and started watching TV. It seemed every woman on the screen was seducing me, attractive or not. I have to mention that these yearnings were not normal, but extraordinarily strong and hard to resist. It was worrisome. A few nights later, I felt the presence of a naked woman standing next to my bed, close to my face. I knew it was that same desire and lust. It was so real. I couldn't actually see her, yet I could describe her body shape, which is something I had never experienced before. Satan was relentless. He pushed at my weaknesses to try to get me to sin. Just about every night I dreamed of naked women and I would participate, because apparently, at that point, I was not holy in my dreams.

I was driving home from church one Sunday and asked God not to let anything come between Him and me. As soon as I said that last word, the cross on my mirror fell to the floor. God was telling me, "Satan is between us." *(See Photos 10.8 & 10.9)*

I was terrified. I picked it up and the leather cord hadn't broken. It wasn't even unclasped. How could it come up and over my mirror and fall to the floor by itself? I called my pastor and asked him to come to my house. After half an hour, he and his wife came over. I told them what had happened. They were as bewildered as I was. Again we prayed for the Devil to leave me.

A few nights later I had a dream that demons were all around me in the form of humans, to have sex with me.

(Photo 10.8)

I asked, "Are you Christian?"

They answered, "No."

I said loudly, "Is anyone Christian around here?"

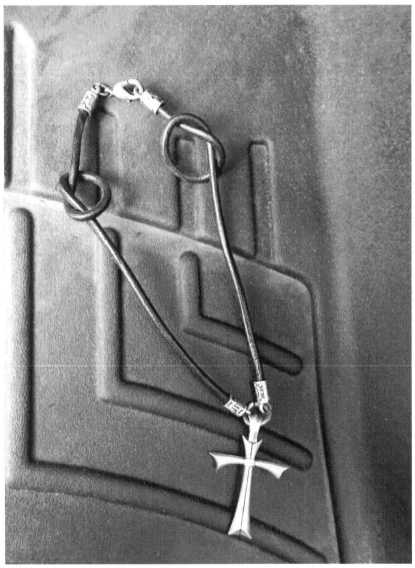

(Photo 10.9)

When I woke up I understood God was showing me the enemy was trying to seduce me and pull me from righteousness.

As time went by the attacks became more severe. While visiting in Big Bear Lake again, I met a lady in a Christian bookstore and began talking about this to her. She gave me an oil that had been prayed over. It was supposed to repel demons. When I got home I put the oil in the shape of a cross in every room and even on my face. The next day, when I came home from work, the guest bathroom door, which is always closed, was now wide open. I took this as them telling me, "We're not going to go away." *(See Photos 10.10 & 10.11)*

One night I strongly felt, God saying, "Why are you afraid of him when I am with you?"

| *(Photo 10.10)* | *(Photo 10.11)* |

I know the intensity of these attacks is in God's hands. After that I had more courage.

Sanctification and More of Satan's Techniques

When gold is to be purified, it goes through extreme heat. God allows humans to endure difficult trials and tests for His own purpose, sanctification.

When I'm not under attack I can tell how pure I've become. The demons have purified me somehow. The more fire I endure, the more pure I become. God tells me He's always with me in the fire.

> *"Your faith will be like gold that has been tested in a fire. And these trials will prove that your faith is worth much more than gold that can be destroyed. They will show that you will be given praise and honor and glory when Jesus Christ returns."*
> *1 Peter 1:7, (C.E.V.)*

In the second and third dreams the mountain was steep to climb, but I did climb it. I worshiped God and brought back blessings (grapes). The mountain represents hardship which in my case is the Devil and his demons, but after each attack I became holier and holier. God permitted them to attack me so I could understand how evil they are. I realized when they wanted to attack me they had to get permission from God. God allowed it for His own purpose for me to be sanctified.

After the dream of the demons trying to seduce me, God made them stop tempting me for lust of the flesh, and they stopped completely after my cross dropped from the mirror to the floor.

However, they merely changed their tactics. I was driving home from work and a whisper from an unclean spirit said, "Worship me." Instinctively, I knew it was Satan. He started to curse at me profanely.

As I watched TV one day I felt Satan's presence touching the hair on my head oh so lightly, just enough to show me he was there. He was doing the same thing to my back, lightly touching. This continued for about a minute. It seems like they enjoy scaring me.

One night I was harassed by Satan at 2:00 a.m. It made me so angry that I told him, "If you think I'm afraid of your ugly face, you're wrong. Even if you appeared here right now, I wouldn't be afraid of you. God knows the outcome of this battle and I will win."

Once I said, "Get away from me. In the name of Jesus of Nazareth I command you to get away." They didn't. They had no fear. I could tell they were high-ranking demons, not low.

"Jesus said, 'Simon, listen to me! Satan has demanded the right to test each one of you, as a farmer does when he separates wheat from the husks.'" Luke 22:31, (C.E.V.)

"When you cross deep rivers, I will be with you, and you won't drown. When you walk through fire, you won't be burned or scorched by the flame." Isaiah 43:2, (C.E.V)

The Devil just wants to harass me and take me away from God. Anytime I go to church, as soon as I get close, it starts to attack me as if it sees where I'm going. I believe these creatures are everywhere following me around, aware of everything that is happening in my life.

Isolation is another one of Satan's techniques to move you away from God and toward him. I mentioned something about demons to my ex-wife, but she didn't want to hear about it. One of my clients didn't come back either. I even noticed my pastor became more distant. They are afraid and want to change the subject. They don't want to know or hear about Satan. That's how we are. The spirits have that advantage.

Satan is tremendously powerful. He can do things we cannot comprehend. He will bring up all your past sins and make you feel guilty and never let you forget them. He knows them all because he was with you when you sinned.

He and his demons understand every language. They know anatomy, and physiology, and how to tamper with details. They breed demonic fear in a person that is unexplainable. They play with your mind and most of the time they win. We have to sleep, but they do not so they don't get tired.

In my case, they know my personality, my likes and dislikes. They know my favorite curse words and use them against me every day. They whisper in our ears, play games and make us feel powerless.

Chapter 12

A Dream of God and Me

Whenever I think of God I picture Him as an extremely handsome, clean looking, middle-aged man. His hair is perfectly combed to the side. He is beautifully clothed in a long white robe and sandals. He is sitting in His office in Heaven viewing all of humanity, trying to create harmony. He isn't necessarily smiling, but has a look of confidence. Like a truly awesome father would have.

God gave me a dream of Him and me. It was very short, only a few seconds. In this dream He had the same face I had pictured in my mind. We were walking on the sidewalk. There was no one there, but God and me. I turned to look at Him and said, "You are my God, you created me. Oh, my God, I am walking with you!" He was looking at me and smiling.

God reaffirmed, "I'm proud of you. I love you. I understand. I am close to you. Do not stop. I am walking with you." He's so happy and proud of me because I am obeying Him. I lightly touched His shoulder and I kissed it. He accepted me doing this. He was so pleased and confident, telling me He knows I'm going to be okay, and I am a good, obedient child.

When I woke up I felt He was telling me He loves me and this is just the fire I have to go through because all sin must be separated from me. I was so happy I had the dream, but the enemy wouldn't leave me alone. It was telling me God didn't forgive me.

I went to Mammoth Mountain about five hours away from my home just for a rest. Satan was harassing me the whole way. Same old games, "God did not forgive you" and breathing fear into me. When I got to Mammoth that night, I was driving around looking for my reserved condo. The radio was on and the preacher said, "God did not bring you all this way to leave you." As soon as I heard that, I noticed the cross on my mirror had moved yet again. It had come off the bar and was sitting on the left end of the mirror, but didn't fall. *(See Photo 12.1)*

God was telling me, "I am here with you" and giving me reassurance that He's not going to leave me. He was validating what I was hearing on the radio. When I experience a new miracle, however, it never gets easier to accept or understand because it's a supernatural process.

I heard one pastor say, "The holier the life we have, the more severe the attacks from Satan." After a while I wasn't afraid of him anymore and I would respond back, "Just go to Hell! Leave me alone!"

(Photo 12.1)

Chapter 13

God's Grace Verses Satan's Evil

When I pray I asked God to empty Hell of humans and fill it with Satan and his demons. I did not love human beings in the past the way I do today. Loving mankind had become a burden to me. This new agape love comes from God. I don't want anyone to go through what I am going through.

I wish people could learn the lesson not to sin and walk with God. If anyone would experience what I had, they wouldn't pursue any sin at all because they would know the Devil is behind it. I pray God gives wisdom to everyone. God's desire is for no one to be destroyed, not even a single person. Satan wants no one to be saved.

Unfortunately, the problem is that we don't all know God and we certainly don't know Satan. God's world is holy and pleasant, but Satan's is the opposite. Many people don't believe Satan even exists. This is what he wants. He will be more successful then.

I know the Devil will be defeated as he was at Calvary. Yet, because of his disgusting nature, he enjoys seeing me be tortured so he keeps after me. He's like a bucket of black paint. You can't extract one drop of white paint from it. His intentions are never good. God is like a bucket of white paint with no black. God's intentions are always good.

I just want you to understand the nature of evil because in the end, the choice is either God or the Devil. Do you want to be in God's favor or Satan's? I know those who believe in Jesus Christ are in favor of God the Father, but sadly those who don't know Him are in sin.

I wasn't raised Christian. Most of my life I was Muslim. Why am I so insistent to portray this as the right way to salvation? It's because I love you, and I know it to be so. I've experienced this spiritual world first hand.

In the second dream, the woman told me the mountain was extremely hard to climb. Yet, I managed to climb to the peak and worship God. God again used the mountain analogy in the third dream. I was to face hardships and extreme difficulties, but would be unharmed. I was given blessings symbolized by the grapes.

I love God so much. He saved me from eternal Hell and promised to make me holier and He did. He showered me with blessings from Heaven on that wonderful night, and Satan saw it all.

When Adam and Eve disobeyed God they had to leave the garden because they became sinners, thereby separated from God. Their children were born as sinners because their parents sinned. We descended from Adam and Eve so we, too, are sinners.

Before the crucifixion of Jesus Christ, people would sacrifice a lamb to God for forgiveness of their sins. God forgave them, but they continued to sin. This made God sad. So He decided to send His Son, Jesus Christ to this world. It was Jesus' mission to be put on the cross and die to pay the price for our sins. He was a perfect lamb to be sacrificed for the salvation of all people. Anyone who believes in Jesus Christ, the Son of God, will be adopted by God as His own child and allowed into Heaven to be with Him forever.

He will live within you. Ask Him to purify you. Obey His commandments and you will become worthy and holy. This is the way to salvation. There is no other way. I am pleading with you to ask God to show you and He will. I want all of us to be saved and no one destroyed. I'm telling you through my own experience what I know to be true. If we understand who God is, we will pursue love, not hate. We will always follow God, not His biggest enemy.

When I feel under attack I tell Satan, "Leave me, you trash!"

Once I experienced the voice of the Holy Spirit telling me in my language, Farsi, "This 'trash' is actually purifying you." You see how God explains things to me? God wants me to understand what's happening.

One day I decided to go back to Big Bear Lake and went to the same lodge as before. I rented a room by myself in a very pretty area where I usually sit and read the Bible. I was reading the Old Testament.

In the Book of *Deuteronomy 23:1 God said, "If a man's private parts have been crushed or cut off, he cannot fully belong to the Lord's people."*

I was nervous and fearful and started talking to God. "God you know I had surgery and because of this are you trying to tell me you reject me or don't love me or do you still love me? It's in the Old Testament, you said it, but do you still love me?"

Nighttime came and around 9:00 p.m. I went outside my room to enjoy the fresh air. I noticed on the second floor, a woman standing all by herself. I didn't want to be there so I came inside. I went to my bed and started watching my program on my laptop.

About five minutes later somehow I wanted to go back outside. I went toward the door and tried to open it, but it would not open. When I looked down, I saw that the long runner rug had moved on top of the small floor mat crossways in front of the door, so I physically could not open the door. I was shocked, so I sat and started praying. *(See Photos 13.1 & 13.2)*

I asked, "Is that you Lord?"

I didn't even see the rug move. I was thinking of what happened. I had gone through surgery and asked if He still loved me. So then I felt more comfortable and God said, "I love you regardless of your surgery." I believe nothing happens without God's permission. My surgery was His plan for His own reasons. So I took a picture of the rug before and after only for myself. When I got home from Big Bear, I noticed the little magnetic cross that was stuck to my safe had moved to a different spot, again confirming that this was Him. I took

(Photo 13.1)

another photo, but didn't know I would write a book one day. I just wanted to keep the memories of these supernatural events and my walk with God. *(See Photos 13.3 & 13.4)*

(Photo 13.2)

(Photo 13.3)

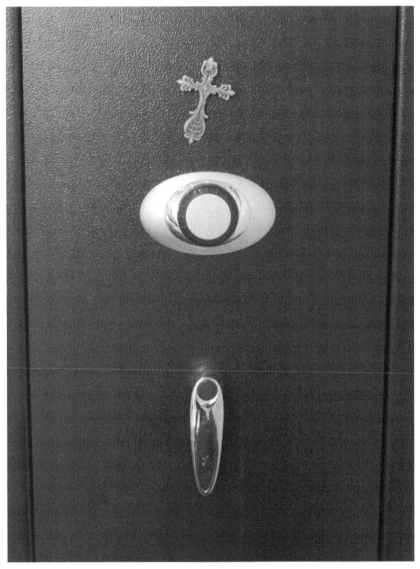

(Photo 13.4)

Chapter 14

My Love For God

I feel very close to God. I am in love with my Creator. I love Him so much I can't understand it. I try telling people, but they can't comprehend it either. They respect and like God as our Creator, but don't seem to have a powerful love for Him.

I used to go with pretty women no matter what, but I love God so much I don't want to do anything to upset Him. I just love Him. It's impossible to put into words. I cry for Him two or three times a day. It's an unexplainable love. I would do anything for Him which is why I don't want to sin. I love Him, I love Him, I love Him.

When I worship God I tell Him how much I love Him and I ask Him, "Do you really love me the way I love you?"

I hear His response, "Mohammad, I love you way more that you love me. I am greater than you and my love is way greater than your love, because you are human and I am your Creator." It's so amazing to me. So sweet.

Even though I've never seen God, my love for Him is strong and becomes stronger every day. I told Him, "I want to be with you. Sometimes I wish I could hold your feet and put my head on them and fall asleep where I know I am safe and no one can bother me."

I wish He could come to my house and be with me, give me advice and bless me. I would kiss His hands and feet and thank Him.

I think of Him every moment. Once I was crying hard, so moved by my love and appreciation for Him. I looked at the cross on my bedroom wall and said, "Lord you know how much I love you in my heart. I want to hold and kiss you, and look at you, and tell you Father, that I love you, but I can't, because you are Spirit." I then fell asleep and had a wonderful dream.

Dream of A White Dove

I dreamed my daughter and her mom were in a room. My daughter said, "Come see this white Dove on the floor, Dad!" I saw how incredibly beautiful it was. I delicately picked it up and held it in my hands. I looked at it tenderly. It was so cute and adorable, fluffy and round and it had a soulful, wise look in its eyes. It was gazing at me and I just wanted to kiss it. I brought it closer to my face and I did. I kissed it. I felt the Dove was just waiting for me to do that. This was the end of the dream. *(See Photo 14.1)*

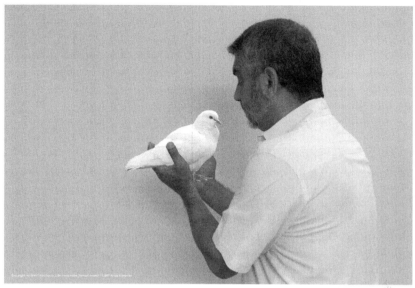

(Photo 14.1)

Now I understand God's deep love for us. The meaning of the dream was crystal clear. That was God.

Before my baptism I met a popular actor who came to my baptism in Zuma. I spoke with him from time to time. We went to lunch once and I explained all my experiences of God. He was very surprised, but he did believe me. He started to come to me for haircuts. Now he's my friend and my client. He told me, "The reason you experienced all this is because you have God in your heart not just your mind." One day he texted me and said he was very impressed with my story.

He said, "I would like to record your experiences in my studio."

I said, "Okay."

We set a time and date. At the end of that day I went to the back of my barbershop and prayed, "Lord I'm going in front of a camera, help me." I was supposed to wash the dirty towels in my shop that day. I had a friend living in my guesthouse who called me while I was on the freeway. He asked if I would go rent a snake for a clogged pipe.

I went to the laundromat and put my towels in washers. I had a half hour to come back to put them in the dryer so I went to the hardware store and rented a snake. I brought it to him then went back to put the towels in the dryer. I returned to my car to sit while they dried. Right away I noticed the cross on my mirror had moved from hanging over the back of the mirror to draping over the front. I got nervous, but kept looking and asked God, "What are you telling me? Should I go with this man and get behind the camera?"*(See Photos 14.2 &14.3)*

(Photo 14.2)   *(Photo 14.3)*

I was uncomfortable. I showed my friend the cross.

He said, "God is trying to tell you something."

I said, "I just want you to see it for yourself."

I called my pastor and told him about this.

He said "God is telling you to go for it," but I understood it as God saying "No don't do it."

Two weeks later my friend sent me a text saying he had to postpone the filming. I told him it was okay, no problem. I was actually disappointed and confused, wondering what God's purpose was here, and why shouldn't I do this and talk about Him.

Chapter 15

Change and Predictions

People who don't believe in Jesus will have to be with Satan forever. This breaks my heart, because I love people. If they could know and believe my story it might help them, but God is the only one who saves.

That's why I say this is God's job, not man's, and the only way He can convince us, is by increasing our wisdom to comprehend Him. God changed me. I'm a new man.

> *"Anyone who belongs to Christ is a new person. The past is forgotten, and everything is new." 2 Corinthians 5:17, (C.E.V.)*

At first, when the demons wanted to make me look bad in front of God, they would make me engage with a naked woman in my dreams. I was not holy then and lost those battles, but I would wake up suddenly and feel shame. I knew the demons were laughing at me, but God was only watching me, not judging me.

I prayed to God, "I am your child, please stop these dreams. I want to be holy when I am dreaming too."

I challenged the Devil, "You don't fight like a man. You fight like yourself, you're small. I challenge you when I'm not sleeping to tempt me." In the past I had been tempted by sexual sin and couldn't resist. But sin isn't pleasant anymore.

In my dream that night, as soon as I was going to engage with a woman, I abruptly woke up and opened my eyes. It meant God was watching my dream. He woke me up. I looked at the cross on my bedroom wall and said, "Father, thank you. I didn't lose the battle."

I went to the bathroom and washed myself with cold water. I went back to bed and slept 20 more minutes, but had another dream. Just before I became intimate with this woman, my eyes opened. God was helping me again.

Satan is working hard, but I pray to God to keep me holy in my dreams. I beg God, and He wakes me up. This is when I actually laugh at Satan saying, "You can't even get me in my dreams anymore because God is helping me. You cannot win this battle, don't you get it?"

See the pattern? Satan wants me to look bad to Holy God. I followed Satan for 58 years and now he has lost me. God knows the intentions of my heart, and that I only want to obey Him and be holy. I am a new creation.

Now before I go to bed, I thank God for what He's doing for me. I understand two things, 1.) The cross is actually God and He's on the wall watching me, even through the suffering of Satan's harassment, and 2.) God is holy and He truly wants me to be holy too. He means it. I really believe this. He is the most holy entity that exists and wants us to be His children. He blesses us with things we don't even understand, or expect, which are wonderful gifts. He pays attention to me and protects me when I'm sleeping.

Sometimes I have no choice, but to put a bag of ice on myself, which is very uncomfortable, but it's better than losing the battle to Satan. I hate Satan and his evilness. I believe God is proud of me. Sometimes when I would take a shower, I'd feel vulnerable because I knew Satan and his demons were watching me. I tried to cover up and at the same time clean myself. After a short time of this though, I felt more comfortable, because God transformed me and I felt secure in His hands again. The Devil hates mankind and he will harass everyone, especially those who walk with God.

Dream To Write My Book

A few days before Christmas, 2017, I had a dream. I saw a midnight blue sky which had some kind of a glow. I heard a voice from above, the same voice I'd heard the first time, when God said He'd make me holier.

He told me, "Write your book." *(See Image 15.1)*

The dream was about four to five seconds and that was it. That next morning I was bewildered. I couldn't get it out of my mind the whole day.

I don't know how to write a book. I had assumed God didn't want me to share with people in front of camera and now a book? All day I contemplated it and that night, after my

(Image 15.1)

shower I sat next to the fireplace. I asked God if that was Him telling me to write a book. And if it was, then to please find the right people to help me with it. After five minutes I went to my room and noticed the picture on the wall was radically tilted. Right away I knew it was God. *(See Photo 15.2)*

(Photo 15.2)

His answer was, "Yes, that was me, and write the book."

I said, "Please introduce me to the right people and show me how." Then I was thinking and said, "Lord, remember my request in Big Bear about eight months ago?" I had written a note in my phone, "Father, I would like to write a book about you, and I want the book to be the #1 seller book in all of history. In Jesus' name Amen." *(See Screenshot 15.3)*

115

❮ Notes

Father,I am going to write a book about you. Please help me through this process and let me find the right people for this purpose.
Father,let this book to be the best seller in history.
In Jesus name

    Amen

(Screenshot 15.3)

I just said it, but didn't really mean it or think about it. I had asked without even thinking. It would be such a bold request. So many books in the world have been best-sellers.

Then I asked God, "If I write the book, will it be a #1 best-seller? And, if it is, then show me a sign." He didn't give me one, but three.

Thursday nights the whole neighborhood puts their trash cans out on the curb and the next day the city comes to do pick up. There is a green one for garden trimmings, a black one for the landfill, and blue for recycling. But when I had bought this house, there were two blue ones here.

Thanksgiving, 2017, I had ordered a small scooter to ride in my neighborhood. I kept the scooter box for a month just in case anything went wrong with it. I decided to get rid of the box that night. I put it in one of the blue containers and rolled it to the street. I put the trash there also (the black container) and I went to bed. In the morning I woke up, showered and went outside. The black container was empty. The blue one with the big box in it was still full. So I brought the black container inside the yard, but the blue container stayed on the street.

I worked all day and recalled my request for God to give me a sign. I went home after work and as soon as I got in front of my house, I saw there were two blue containers in the middle of my driveway. I wondered who put this blue one here. I parked my car on the street, and started to push the container back into the yard. Then I remember asking God for a sign. It was in front of the driveway, there was only one, but now two! *(See Photos 15.4 & 15.5)*

117

(Photo 15.4)

(Photo 15.5)

I started crying and said, "Lord you're confirming your promise." I live alone. Who would do this? The second blue bin was about 25 feet away from the driveway. It was empty anyway. I was thinking, Lord when I ask you things, you respond. How can I not love you? How can I stop thinking of you or ignore you? Father, you are amazing. Why are you so close to me and answering all my prayers?

The next day in my pill container there was an extra red pill in each daily compartment along with my other pills. But I always put only one red one in each compartment, not two. (*Photos 15.6 & 15.7*)

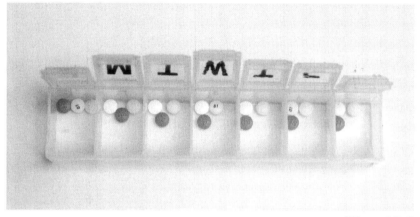

(Photo 15.6)

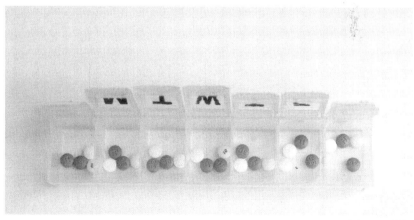

(Photo 15.7)

I said, "Lord, I know you are confirming it. I know, Lord. I know it's you."

A few days later on my way to work I was thinking of all of these experiences with God. I had stopped at a red light when I felt a breeze hit me even though the windows were rolled up and the doors shut.

I said, "Lord, I know, I know. I believe you!"

So, three times He confirmed his promise. The date of the dream was 12/09/17. So here I am, and here is my book.

It was getting close to Christmas and I was listening to Christmas music, especially the songs Silent Night and Oh Holy Night. I was becoming more and more in love with God. I'd get goosebumps because I felt His love for me.

Close to Christmas Eve I told Jesus, "You know how much I love you, how Satan is bothering me and how lonely I am. I have no one to be with me for Christmas. Would you be with me? Show me a sign that you will be with me this Christmas and that you love me so I'm not by myself."

Christmas Eve was Sunday night. I had a manger scene with statues in my front yard next to the door. I plugged it in along with the lights on my trees.

I said, "Tonight I'm leaving the Christmas lights on."

The night before Christmas Eve at 3:00 a.m. I woke up and could see all the neighbors' Christmas lights were turned off so I unplugged mine too along with the manger scene. I fell asleep. I woke up and went to work until 4:30 p.m. When I left work, I went to the market and bought flowers for God for Christmas. As soon as I drove into my driveway I saw the manger scene was plugged in and lit up! I sat in the car just looking at this holy manger scene. (See *Photo 15.8*)

(Photo 15.8)

I had unplugged it last night. I cried in my car. I knew God was saying, "I love you and I am with you this Christmas." I can't explain how close God can be. He came in the form of a Dove and allowed me to hold Him and kiss Him. It was so adorable and precious. He confirmed His promise by showing me miracles. He lit up the manger scene to prove to me He is with me and He loves me. Should I really disobey such a pleasant, lovely, wonderful God? I will forever adore Him, love Him, obey Him, and worship Him. I pray for everyone to experience God the way I do.

121

Dream of the Day of Justice

Sometime after Christmas, I had a dream that I was in a room with a big window frame, but no glass for the window. I could see only ground and sky. Suddenly, I saw hundreds of thousands of horses descending from the sky coming toward the earth. There were brightly colored angels riding these horses, but they weren't sweet ones, not the type to give nice messages to people. They were warriors with spears. Somehow I saw red around them and I knew it meant war and the last day. I looked up and said, "Oh, it's God!"

I got scared and backed away from the window, hoping they'd disappear. But I went back and there were even more coming down. On the other side of room, was a door. I went outside and looked up. I saw even more of these angels and horses. Many had already reached the ground. Somehow each angel was coming for a certain person on earth.

I was watching them and noticed the way their horses landed from the sky onto the ground. It was so realistic and amazing. There were a few people in front of the building standing in line waiting for their angels. Therefore, I stood up next to them. I was the last one in line. I was looking straight ahead, not at the angels. Nobody else was looking at them either. I believe because of the fear. Suddenly, I noticed an enormous horse with a very big angel riding on it. It came almost in front of my face. I turn my head to the right side to look at him and as I did the dream abruptly ended.

God is telling us to stay away from evil, to repent, and come to Him. He will forgive you and not remember your sins anymore. There is a justice day, and it will come soon.

Chapter 16

My Testimony and The Struggle

I believe God has a special plan for me. When I started walking with God, the Devil and his demons began attacking me. I knew they didn't like me. They can read our minds. They are familiar with our personalities. They know all our sins because they were with us all along. They try to make us feel that it is okay to sin. That is why many people commit sins daily. They are a slave to it. I knew a woman who had the need to engage with men many times a day, every day. I didn't understand that these were demons attacking this poor woman. These creatures increase the craving for sex and breed this into us.

Every one of them has a specific job. One increases sexual craving while another intensifies greed and jealousy. There is one who glorifies substance abuse and another who encourage violence. There is a demon that breeds fear and depression in you which causes some people to commit suicide. Another one is to give you doubt. One just curses at God and you. Why do you think people are compelled to kill each other for no reason at all? These evil ones go to any length to deceive you. They have endless energy and no decency.

The demons know they have more power than humans. We can't conquer them without God's on our side. They know all languages in the world. I'm sure these creatures have different ranks and are skilled at different levels. I believe there are the same levels of evil as there are holiness. They're extremely jealous of God. It seems like they have no fear of Him.

God has promised they will all go to Hell and they know it, but still they continue to spread evil. We are human, and we have to rest and sleep, but demons don't need sleep and always have energy.

Many people come to Christianity and are baptized, but they haven't had all the experiences I've had. Why did I see Heaven open up? How many can say they have heard God's voice and received His messages? Why am I experiencing all these supernatural miracles? One thing I know for sure, I am a changed man. I have this wonderful holiness from Jesus Christ my Lord and my Savior.

These demons know I'm walking with God and they know it is real. I'm not playing anymore, which is why they attack me. They hate me and I hate them. I'm not afraid of them, because I have God and He confirmed that He is with me. He loves His sheep and no one can take them away from Him.

God said, "I would never leave nor forsake you." Deuteronomy 31:6, (C.E.V.)

Jesus said, "I am good shepherd" John 10:11, (C.E.V.)

There is a continual war between the Devil and me. Some nights I have scary dreams. When I wake up it's clear Satan is playing games again. They vibrate the muscles in my body to give me the message, "It's us. Ha, ha, ha!"

They are always confirming that it is them, and I understand that confirmation. But God has already told me the outcome. I know I am in the middle of the fire, but I also know this fire will not burn me.

He said, "Between you and me there is a mountain which is tough to climb, but you will, and you will come to me and I will bless you." And He did, Nov 4, 2015 at about 9:00 p.m. when He opened up the Heavens and blessed me. If He promises something, you can count on it. Trust Him.

I pray to God every day to bless everyone. God is the Creator and He loves His creation. Unfortunately, Satan will come and some people will go with him. That will be a tragic day. I'm asking every one of you from the bottom of my heart to pray for each other. Don't sin and ask God's forgiveness. We should love and pray for each other, because we are all humans.

Someday we'll have to leave this world whether you like it or not, healthy or sick, wealthy or poor. Some believe if we do right, we go to Heaven and if we do wrong, we go to Hell. But I know we can't go to God just by doing right things because humans cannot be righteous. The only way to receive this is by accepting Jesus Christ, then Holy God will come and live within us. He is the one to make us righteous. This is a gift from Him.

After I die, what will happen to my spirit if I'm by myself without my God? I won't know where to go, but now I have God in me and He knows the way to His house. He will take me. I will behave like God and think like God. I'm going to associate with Him and His angels in a holy place. If I am going to live with God, I must be holy. I have to be cleansed by Him and away from sin. How can I live with Holy God if I still choose to sin? Sin will separate us.

But how can I go live with God after all those years of wrong behavior? That's correct I associated with women and used profanity. I lied and did much more. But God says He will cleanse us and separate us from sin, and from the desires of this world. I believe one of the ways God cleanses me is by the fire I endure most of the time, which is from Satan himself.

These unclean spirits know how to play games with our minds and they begin with little thoughts like, "Mohammad it's okay to look at women, can you imagine a wife like that? There's nothing wrong with having a wife," but quickly he takes me to a different level. I just say "I don't need a wife. I need God. Go to Hell, Devil."

Since we are all sinners, Satan is always present. I know everywhere I go the evil ones are with me. If I'm drinking water, eating or sleeping, they are watching me and trying to spoil my enjoyment. They will do anything to disturb you, irritate you and make you uncomfortable, more so when you're tired. They know if you didn't sleep well you will be more vulnerable. The major things Satan uses to seduce us are sex and money. Sadly, most of the time, he succeeds. Humans are in love with these things. That's why so many of us lose the battle.

The answer is to pray asking God to open our eyes to Satan's tricks. Tell Him, "I'm in love with a temporary pleasure and I know it's pulling me from you. Please give me power and help me to resist." When God sees that you want to get closer to Him, He will reach out His loving hand and help you.

Even now, that I know I am truly walking with God, I pray every night, "God clean my eyes and my heart even more. If there's any hate, envy, greed, lust, or jealousy, please take it away. Father, I want to forgive everyone and you know this. I want to be clean, holy, and pure like you. Sanctify me even more. Let me help others, Father. Please exchange all these wrong desires with your wholesome ones. Clean us, make us holy."

Unfortunately, even though Satan is actually afraid of God, he continues to pursue his evil plan. Seems like he has no brain and thinks of no consequences. The Devil knows Gods plan for me, and he wants to sabotage it.

He's always reminding me of my sins and in return I keep telling him, "Do you remember my baptism at Zuma Beach?"

He wants to make me weak, and sad, and removed from God. His harassment is so obvious that as soon as I go to bed, he makes a vibration on my legs, and I have to keep stretching them so I can sleep. He always wants me depressed and fearful. But God tells us He didn't give us a spirit of fear. Therefore, all Satan can do is harass us and no more.

God won't let him do more than our limits. I'm sure these demons can even betray each other. If something happens Satan will run away and abandon his own demons. He cannot be loyal, even to his demon army. When we are in sin we won't

129

see or feel any of these attacks. Why should the enemy attack us when we are already doing what they want?

As soon as we go to God and have a longing to live with Him and not sin, then we feel the attacks more acutely. I understand that Satan is powerful, but it is a power he received from God and it comes back to God as nothing, like a drop of water in the ocean. He has no class, wisdom, moral character, feeling, heart. He loves to kill, use profanity, hates everyone, and he has bad intentions. That's why we see people in this world who have these characteristics. They belong to Satan.

This is an uncomfortable subject for me to talk about, but because I love you I want you to understand the nature of evil spirits.

One night I woke up and saw a demon sitting on my bed. It looked like a man's silhouette. I couldn't see any face or other details. He was smaller than me. I looked at him and he left the bed and disappeared. I saw the same thing twice. Many nights I wake up with an extreme heat sensation all over my body and push the blanket away, yet the temperature is only 69 or 70 degrees. Even at work I can feel that heat and I see sweat on my palms.

I get moody. The demons watch every detail of what I do. They create vibration in my entire body that weakens me. When I go to church or read the Bible, I sometimes fall asleep. I don't know if it is Satan himself, but if it is why am I so important that he bothers with me?

One day I bought flowers for God and when I got outside the store, I felt something like a razor blade inside my belly. It was a terrible, demonic feeling, very painful. Satan responds right away to any Godly deed. It may be hard to believe, but it is real. He is a mean spirit.

Once I was just passing through a department store and noticed the ladies lingerie section. I wanted to avoid it so I went down a different aisle.

I bragged to Satan and said, "See how holy I am?" He immediately caused the razor blade pain in my belly again. For two days I felt terrible.

They watch me like a camera, turned on all day and all night, seven days a week. They revile holiness, so they harass people who walk closely with God. If I'm around many people, the unclean spirits don't care about the others. Their focus is on me and they are aware of everything happening around me. Even if I make a phone call, they know what is going on.

Most of the time there is a wheezing sound in my left ear. When it gets louder, their activities become stronger. They are trying harder to make me feel miserable and seem to enjoy seeing me suffer. They cause a vibration in my abdomen making my muscles tighten. It's a strange demonic feeling, something any human would reject. All I could do was pray.

Some nights I feel something pinching my abdomen. It wakes me up and I can't sleep for another two hours. When I do fall asleep the same thing happens again. They are trying to make me tired and when I'm tired the attacks are stronger. If I run into any small problems and get nervous, they magnify this feeling. If I have a medical issue, they intensify the fear. They just want me to live in fear, and make my life miserable. Sometimes when I'm at the coffee shop, I feel that place is dark and narrow and I want to leave as soon as I can. They play with my mind and my nerves.

I remember one night it was very late, maybe 2:00 a.m. Someone knocked on the front door quite hard and it woke me up, but I didn't go to the door because I just knew it was them.

In the beginning of all of this, I was extremely fearful, but it has been over two years of harassment now, so I'm not afraid anymore. I keep telling them, "Even if you show your ugly face, I won't be afraid. Go ahead, give me your best shot you little bastards."

God told me not to be afraid because He's always with me. Sometimes when I wake up with a bad demonic feeling and see the cross on my wall I question God saying, "You're here watching all this and yet you do nothing about it? Don't you love me?"

However, I understand He's telling me, "This is the fire, the test and you will be fine. Your faith will be strong and after you pass the test, you will have a pleasant life."

One night, I decided to get more information about demons. So I went to the internet and listened to a pastor explain about these creatures and how to cast them out. There were a few steps which were mostly prayers.

He warned, "Don't do it by yourself."

I said, "I'm tired of this and I'm going to pray tonight and get rid of them now."

So I started these steps by myself and I felt the room was full of demons. The more I prayed, the more exhausted I became. I was so weak I had to lie down, so I wouldn't fall down, but they didn't go away. I was so drained I fell asleep.

Chapter 17

I Am A Christian

In the book of Daniel 3:1-38, three Hebrew teens, Shadrach, Meshach, and Abednego refused to bow before King Nebuchadnezzar's statue. The King wanted an explanation. They said they do not bow to anyone but God.

The King demanded they be put in a fiery furnace and increase the temperature to seven times hotter. Everyone watched as the three were bound and thrown into the furnace. Then they noticed a fourth person in the fire, who was an angel of God. The King told them to come out of the fire. He saw they were not burned and said he'd seen a fourth person protecting them and praised God, "Who sent His angel and rescued His servants!"

I know God's in my room every night watching me in my sleep and my dreams, because Satan is able to give me nightmares and unholy dreams. God protects me and is in charge of everything.

I am not the same man I was before Satan's attacks. I feel more purified. I know it is difficult for most of you to believe and understand. But I simply cannot do anything unholy, and this is something that amazes me. My nature has changed and I'm a truly different person. This is why I believe that during my baptism, the old Mohammad died, but I didn't feel or understand it at the time. Still, the new Mohammad was born. As time went by, I started noticing this, and today, I'm a new creation who loves and obeys God.

There's no evil in my heart and I love all human beings. I love all of you, and, yet I don't even know you. It doesn't matter who you are, what color your skin is, where you live on the planet, in the forest, the mountains or if you are rich or poor. I want you all to go to God.

God told me that He would make me holy and now I know what that is, what being a holy man means. I love reading my Bible, praying and talking to my Father in Heaven.

God is the greatest power, and nothing can go against Him. He created the universe, Heaven, and Earth; everything you see and don't see. Satan did not create anything because he is not a creator, he is just a fool. Satan was created just like we were, by God. Unfortunately, he wants me to worship him. I don't understand why he demands this, because his creator is my creator also.

"Why do you expect me to worship you?" I ask him.

This is the way he thinks. He is jealous of God and wants to take over His throne. This is why he's going to Hell and why he is a fool.

Before my baptism, I didn't know much about God and His power. Since then God has given me a lot of knowledge. When I think about the past, and how easy it was to sin, I am ashamed. I was breaking God's commands daily. Yet, I had no animosity toward Him. I never told God I was against Him. I just didn't know better because of my lack of wisdom. If I was not against God though, how come I kept breaking His commands? I realize I simply didn't know who God was. I only knew His name and that He was the Creator, just like many people. Yet, they don't want to have anything to do with Him. I thought I knew the meaning of holiness, but I really didn't at all. In order to understand it, you must have the experience of holiness.

Today when I think about myself, I have the same body, voice, and I walk the same, but I don't have the same nature. What happened to me? What power transformed me? Is it possible that human nature changes? Is it the work of the human or from above? What is it?

Not only can I not commit sin, but I don't even want to think about it. Today it is impossible. I hate my past. It was a scary time, like walking toward fire. At any moment I could get into the fire and destroy myself more and more.

I know that Satan is always around sinners. The poor, unfortunate sinners don't believe it, or understand it. I know when God called me and chose me, He knew I was going to commit all these sins, and break all of His commands. Yet, He put a halt to it.

In His mind He thought, You will do this until age 58, but after that, you will become my child. I will accept you and change you. I will bless you and I will love you.

Most people believe that God doesn't love them because of their daily sins, I know they are wrong. God doesn't love what you do, but He loves YOU. Remember, He promised to bless me when I was in sin, so He always was with me and loved me, but was not happy with my behavior. Go to Him and you will understand. He has always loved you even when you were sinning. God loves His creations and humans are His masterpieces.

When you believe in Jesus Christ, He will cleanse you. You won't understand how this is all happening. You just notice changes in your desires, your ways of thinking, how you treat others, and so much more. I don't even recall the last time I used profanity. Somehow it just wasn't part of me after my baptism. I said to God, "Oh, my God, I don't use foul language anymore." The difference amazed me.

After about a year, though, I noticed I still had some jealousy in my heart. I prayed to God, "Father, Father, please take this desire from me. Bless me with good desires." Today, after three years, I feel a huge difference in myself.

Jesus said, "5. I tell you for certain that before you can get into God's Kingdom, you must be born not only by water, but by the Spirit. 6. Humans give life to their children yet only God's Spirit can change you into a child of God." John 3:5-6. (C.E.V.)

Only God can make your spirit become alive, and when it does, you will hear and understand holy messages. You can have the ability to see holy miracles from God. Even when you worship Him, you do it in the highest way. That's what He expects from us, to worship Him truly from the bottom of our hearts with the purest desire. It's not a job to worship Him, it's a delight. When you look at the sky and say, "Father, I love you," you will hear His answer which is, "I love you even more."

> *"23. But a time is coming and it is already here! Even now the true worshipers are being led by the Spirit to worship the Father according to the truth. These are the ones the Father is seeking to worship Him. 24. God is Spirit, and those who worship God must be led by the Spirit to worship Him according to the truth." John 4:23-24, (C.E.V.)*

God wants us to be with Him forever in His beautiful Holy City which is Heaven. If you believe that Jesus Christ is the Son of God and died on the cross for our sins, then you will be saved from eternal Hell. It is simple, but impossible for some to believe.

Yet, if I'm supposed to live with God, but I still have the craving to sin, which is of this world and is Satan's wish, how can I go to Heaven and live with God? I must be clean and pure like Him. But I cannot do it by myself. I'm not able. Only God can do that. So I pray for Him to help me and cleanse me from past sins. This cleansing process begins right after accepting Jesus Christ and asking Him to come into your heart. It says it in the Bible. I know this, because I felt it.

God will see you as His righteous child. I am righteous now because He is in me. How can I sin when He's in me? All these things happening to me are called "sanctification" in the Bible. It is the process to make one holy. This process will continue until I am separated from my body. Glorification is the final removal of sin at the end times. I don't know much about glorification because I'm not there yet. But I do know the Holy Spirit will take me to Heaven. At times I can actually feel the joy of Heaven. God confirms all these feelings and beliefs so I have no doubt.

I pray that what He has done for me He will do for all mankind.

Chapter 18

God Is Great

Our Creator loves us. God wants to have a relationship with all of us, but He is gentle and non-intrusive. However, Satan and his demons can come running to my house like wild donkeys, without my permission. God is polite. He is knocking, open the door. I have a picture of Jesus knocking on a door. The door has no handle on the outside. This door is your heart. Only you can open it from the inside and invite Him in. According to the Bible, don't shut the door in His face. The problem is, if we shut the door again and again, we won't ever understand who He is. He is sweeter than sugar. He is kind, wise, powerful, and capable. He is our Creator, and He loves all of us. I hope you understand.

Sometimes when I think about this I wonder, *Am I actually going to live in the city that God lives in? Am I going to be His neighbor? If so, will I be able to talk to Him?*

I just want to be with Him. It's so joyful. I can't explain it. There is nothing like the joy and the love of God. It's not like human love. It's very different. I wish this for everyone.

Why do you think God called me? It is because He didn't want me to be destroyed. I hope many people, by reading this book, will understand and go to God and be saved based on my experience and testimony. This is another reason why I believe Satan is so against me. The Devil knows the degree of my faith and he hates it. I know God can do incredible things to make His children understand, but God has His own way of doing things. In the past, I had a different faith, but now I found God somewhere else. In my book I have written all the details of my life to show you the Way. It is from my heart to yours.

Why do you think as soon as God gave me the wisdom to understand, I baptized my daughter and stepdaughter? It is because I love them. My highest prayer is for the whole world to be baptized. I wish all these words had divine power and could go into your heart to make you comprehend and believe. I want all of us to live with God in Heaven. I also want the Devil and his demons go to their own place, which is Hell. I've never written a book before and I'm not a professional writer, but I feel God channeling these words through me.

I can never forget the night He spoke to me and told me He would change me. Some nights I go to that spot on the sidewalk, stop, and find Him. I walk to the place where the blessings came down and stare at the sky where Heaven is located. I know He's watching me from Heaven as I gaze at Him from earth. Then I go to the third spot where I had the vision I was enormously wealthy with blessings. Some houses' front doors are actually facing Heaven and they don't even know it. They may never understand this, the same way a lot of people won't believe and understand Jesus is the Lord.

God is close to us all, but people don't want to know Him. They distract themselves from seeing Him.

Today, I have more respect for humans. In the past, I wanted to answer evil with evil, and I couldn't forgive everyone 100%. However, now I am very different. I know God will answer all my prayers. I am so far away from my old life.

One day I heard God's voice tell me, "You received your salvation." He said it in Farsi.

God was trying to bring me comfort. Another time I was thinking of insulting Satan. A few minutes later I heard God tell me this is, "Not the way." He was telling me it was the wrong way to fight against Satan. God is polite and a gentleman and I understand this.

God witnesses every moment of my life. I have done a lot of wrong things. Many people betrayed me and left me. But God called me, embraced me, forgave me, and blessed me. Now I am spiritually wealthy. This is why I don't want to sin or make any mistakes. I don't want distance from God. God doesn't expect too much. He just says to live right and be holy – don't sin.

Every time I talk, He listens. He has given me things I never dreamed of, and all these gifts came from Heaven. They will never be damaged, spoiled, or parish and no one can take them away from me. This wealth is a gift you can't buy or receive from anyone but God. How can I betray or disobey Him?

God has the biggest love for us, but unfortunately I did not feel it in the past because I was not close to Him. Just like

145

when a father is away from his child. The child can always stay away from their parents and not feel bad, but the love of parents for their children is different.

God doesn't need us. He has everything. He is wealthy, wise, and generous. So why does He care about us so much? It is because He loves us. He wants to save and bless us. We can't understand His love because we are humans. If we could understand Him He wouldn't be God. We are weak, but He is strong.

Jonah, in the Bible, wanted God to punish the people, but they came to God and God did not want to punish them anymore, but Jonah insisted.

God said, "Do you know how many people and animals I have in that town? Do you know how bad it feels to be punished? They don't know the difference from their right or left hand."

God didn't punish them because they repented and asked for forgiveness so God forgave them. He even cares about His animals. Everything belongs to Him. I believe that even one leaf from the tree can't fall without His permission. He is mighty and proves He is a good God.

He never lies and always fulfills His promises when it is time, not a second sooner or later, but it will happen.

You may say, "If God loves me, how come I don't see these miracles? Why doesn't He talk to me?" I have no answer. That's all I can say. It's just a call for whatever reason. I honestly don't know, but what parent would love one child more than another? God loves all of His children equally. He may not like the child's behavior, but it doesn't mean he doesn't love him. That's how God is. He dislikes all human behaviors, but He still loves us.

There is a story in the Bible, Luke 15:11-32, of the Prodigal son were the father welcomed his son back after he had done wrong to his father. The boy remembered his father's goodness, repented, and returned. The father was very happy and celebrated his return. God is like that.

Then there is the story of the missing lamb. The shepherd left the 99 sheep to find the lost one. After he found it the shepherd was overjoyed. I believe when we are all baptized, the angels in Heaven will celebrate.

> *"I will treat them with kindness, even though they are wicked. I will forget their sins." Hebrews 8:12, (C.E.V.)*

Is God lying? Can He lie? If you believe He doesn't lie, why don't you take advantage of this opportunity and have a blessed life for you and your children. I know that He wants everyone to go to Him.

Chapter 19

A Narrow Path

Some days I complain to God and say, "Father don't you see the Devil is harassing me so much? It's too much for me to handle. Why are you so quiet and don't defend me?"

Yet, I know when God starts a process in someone, He will be with them. He doesn't change the situation; he allows the situation to change the person.

> When Jesus was on the cross he said, *"My God, my God, why have you deserted me?" Matthew 27:46, (C.E.V.)*

God hadn't deserted him. That was God's plan. Before Jesus came to earth, God told him to go into the world, live as a man, spread the Good News and die on the cross for the sins of man. He was to do this to save all of us from eternal Hell.

If God let His Son suffer on the cross, of course He will let me suffer. There is a reason for it, not to be mean, but to cleanse my spirit. Then I can show others the way.

I have a strong feeling that I belong to God, so I do what He asks of me. I don't want to do anything against His will, which still amazes me.

Sometimes when I see a beautiful woman, I instantly turn my head away. I ask myself, *Why? How come I don't look at her?* Then I realize the one who lives in me sees this as a sin and it will get worse if I keep indulging in this behavior. I have to stop it before the Devil gets involved.

The spirit of God is holy and clean, and is definitely separate from these evils. Therefore, His holiness won't let me look. I'm not alone within myself anymore. I have a roommate who is God. When I see some unholy scene, He is watching that scene through me. He doesn't want to see it. Therefore, I turn my head.

But the fact is He is the one turning my head. He did it after my baptism. Remember the story about the TV with the lingerie commercial, when the Holy Spirit turned my face away? He's still doing the same thing, but today I am willing to look away. I'm cooperating with God. This is a fact. The reason my head was turned is He wanted me to understand completely, "It's over Mohammad." I totally got it. No further discussion.

Everything starts with the looking, but if you dwell on looking too long, you will get hooked on a lower level like Joseph in the Bible. The Egyptian woman wanted to get with Joseph, but she was married. Joseph looked away immediately, and that pleased God. Yet, when King David saw the naked woman Bathsheba bathing, he didn't stop and kept looking.

He continued watching, so Satan took him lower, therefore, he wanted to sleep with her. But she was married and her husband was a soldier of King David's. King David started thinking of killing her husband. He sent him to the front lines of the battle and he did get killed. He committed two big sins because he couldn't control himself. He didn't turn his face away which led to sin and he had a man killed. I said before, walking with God is not easy, but if you're willing, He will make it easier. I believe the holier I get, the harder it is to commit sin. He is looking for children to faithfully obey Him.

God's commandments never change, but we are changing. Our culture is changing, and so is our way of living, all for the worse. We are so obsessed with lust and sex, money, power, and greed. Some people are willing to do anything to get rich, which means to obey Satan's desire to be deceitful. We can't party with Satan and go to God for His blessings at the same time. What kind of expectation is that? This life is short and it is a testing place.

How will you feel on the last day of your life when you realize, "Oh, my God, what have I done making all this temporary wealth? I can't take it with me." With more wealth, you have to leave even more behind. I wonder where you are going, Heaven or Hell. What's going to happen to you? Some people believe that day hasn't come yet so they're not worried. Are you one of those?

We live in a world of excesses and greed. I am only one person. Why should I have a three-bedroom house when I need only one bedroom? If I can't eat more than one plate, why order two? If I order two what will happen? I can't eat it all, so I have to throw it in the trash. Now I've wasted my money and the food. It makes no sense. This is nothing but greed dominating me. I wonder how wealthy I will be when I die. But what good does money do for me? It will stay in my bank account and if my children take it they could waste it, because they didn't work hard for it. Therefore, when I get to the last day of my life, I will regret going after all of this wealth.

For so many years I didn't understand this concept. Now I know why. It is because the Devil doesn't want us to get it. However, I know that even at the last moment, if it is God's will, an angel will appear to the lost sheep and make them realize that Jesus is the way to salvation. Just before you die, if you truly believe, you will go straight to Heaven.

Whatever you need, ask God. God won't give you something that is bad for you. Don't ask for a boyfriend or girlfriend. Ask for a husband or wife, because God is holy. If you ask and you don't get it, find what's wrong in your life. Ask God to make you understand what it is that He doesn't agree with. He will show you and help you change.

Without His wisdom we cannot believe for sure if Jesus is the Son of God, or that the Holy Spirit lives within us. God, the Father, is the almighty God. All these things are revealed by the wisdom that He gives to His children. Then they will have no wish to sin and will love God. Temptations will come, but God will help you conquer them.

Many people claim they love God and, yet they sin. In response, God said, "You keep telling me you love me and, yet you disobey me. What kind of love is that? If you love me, obey me."

"If anyone loves me, they will obey me. Then my Father will love them, and He will come to them and live in them." John 14:23, (C.E.V.)

Jesus said, *"Love your enemies." Matthew 5:43, (C.E.V.)*

Forgiveness is one of the highest gifts of God. How is it possible to love someone who tries to hurt you? But God's love is not comprehensible to us because it is so powerful. When you receive His love, you will forgive your enemy. When we become purified we don't feel hate anymore and have no enemies in our heart. This is God's power.

You may ask why God is more active in some than in others who have no spirituality. I believe the answer is because God sees all of our hearts. He knows who wants to be with Him and is willing to cooperate and will sin no more. Before my baptism, I didn't consider myself a real sinner. There were worse people. *I wasn't really bad.* After baptism, I could see how bad I was.

I don't want to judge anyone and tell them they are bad and wrong, because I was worse. Who am I to judge? Only God can judge. All I can do is pray for that person.

Living with God is a clean, straightforward life. It is joyful. Live in the light, not the darkness. I thank God that I have no wish to live as I did in the past. I know now why my ex-wife had to leave. If she hadn't, I wouldn't be at this stage of my life. Because I am by myself now, I only feel God.

Even the best preacher in the world cannot make someone believe. The power of believing comes from God only. I know when people live in sin, the older they get, the more comfortable they become in sin. They can't see what's happening. They are blocked.

I hope after you read this book, you will believe, become children of God, and be baptized. He will forgive you and the Spirit of God will cleanse you. But before we get to Heaven, we have work to do. We have to tell everyone the way to salvation. It's called the Good News of the gospel. When God says, "Love one another" it means you must care for everyone and see them as your own family. Whatever I wish for my own daughter, I should wish for all people, because we are all human beings. We have to support each other through tough times and fight our enemy together.

In the end, I pray for those who lived on earth in the past to be forgiven, and for those who live here now to get wisdom and obey God, because the time is short.

I pray to God to make us realize all of Satan's techniques and strategies to deceive us and destroy us. I not only pray for my family and myself, but for all of humanity. Especially for those who are still in sin and have no clue of the way to salvation. The way to salvation is through no one, but Jesus Christ himself.

Remember...

*If I speak in the tongues of men
and of angels,*

*but have not love, I am a noisy
gong or a clanging cymbal.*

*And if I have prophetic powers,
and understand all mysteries and
all knowledge and if I have all
faith so as to remove mountains,
but have not love,*

I am nothing.

The Back Story

My name is Mohammad. I was born in 1957 in Tehran, Iran. Iran is basically a Muslim country, mostly Shia-Muslim. The main language is Farsi, but in different regions they speak different languages such as Kurdish, Turkish and more.

Unfortunately, it is too often true that when you are born and raised in a Muslim family, you will stay Muslim. It is the same with many other religions. We aren't thinking of other choices. We just believe it in that particular society. The only thing we can do is pray for God to show them the truth.

Where I grew up Iranians were mostly Muslim. We also had a Christian and Jewish minority. Christians lived in one area and didn't associate with Muslims and vice versa. Not because they didn't like each other, it just happened that way. There weren't many churches in Tehran, probably because the religions couldn't meld together easily. I had only one friend who was Christian, but he wasn't practicing it as far as I knew. As a Muslim I used to pray occasionally, but really didn't know God the way I do now. It is my experience that many people claim to know God, but few seem serious about it.

We were middle-class. My father worked for the government. My mother was a housewife and worked hard at home cooking, cleaning and raising us. I have six sisters, I was the only boy. Now I realize my parents were the most precious gift in my life.

We used to play soccer outside. Soccer was a very popular game and just about every neighborhood kid would play. In those days if someone drank alcohol, the whole neighborhood would know because not too many people drank. Movies were our only entertainment, but only occasionally. At the beginning of the movie, they would show a clip of the Shah (Iranian King), play the national anthem, and the whole audience had to stand in respect. It seemed everyone liked the Shah, or maybe they were just afraid to admit the opposite. Eventually, they stopped showing him.

People respected each other a lot more and lived simple lives. There were less pedestrians and cars, and the atmosphere of life was less hectic. During lunchtime when you passed through any neighborhood you could smell the delicious food cooking.

Our neighbors were like family, we knew everything about each other, and we helped one another.

Summers were hot with no air conditioning. I don't know how we did it. Autumn was gorgeous with many different colors of leaves on the trees and an abundance of nourishing rain. I always loved walking in the rain. Winter, however, was quite cold and there was ample snow which gave a fresh, pure face to the city. We would go out and have snowball fights. Our hands got cold, but we didn't care because it was so much fun. Sometimes we had to go on our roofs to shovel the snow off. At times it snowed so much, schools were shut down. This made all the kids happy, of course. More time for exhilarating play in the snow.

Back then, there weren't many TVs as they were expensive and such a new commodity. Plus there were only a couple channels so we watched whatever was on. Telephones were rare as well. I recall my first phone number though. It was only five digits, 57469. Our house had a furnace that ran on kerosene which we had to purchase often. Either it was delivered or we could go get it. We used it for cooking too as we didn't use gas at that time. Things were quite different back then.

The New Year was the first day of spring. Every house would hire people to come and wash the Persian rugs and clean the house. These people had nicknames like Canary or Pigeon, because it was the season of happy springtime. Everyone worked so hard to clean and bring in the New Year. We all wore new clothes and would go visit our eldest family members to show respect. The kids got money as gifts.

I remember when John F. Kennedy was assassinated. Everyone was extremely upset. The whole country liked him very much. In those days, before I went to bed, I used to speak to God and pray for my mom, my dad, my sisters, the whole family, and the neighbors. I asked for no one to get sick and to "Please God, help us all." I was very young though and sometimes I just forgot to pray. I stopped praying after a while.

There were religious processions on the street. I walked next to them and followed them along their route. I thought we were all trying to obey God. We didn't go to the mosque much and weren't very religious, but we did believe in God. In Iran there is a religious month when Muslims fast called Ramadan. They aren't supposed to eat until evening.

When I was little, on those nights my mom would cook extra food for the early morning before sunrise. One hour before that, my dad would wake us all up and turn the radio on and start to pray to God. They would warm the food and we fortified ourselves because of the fast. After an hour we went back to bed because it was still too early. All day, we wouldn't eat. That was a law in Muslim religion in order to keep God satisfied. Of course, those people with health issues had to eat. Restaurants would cover the windows with curtains to not tempt anyone.

In public we couldn't drink water, chew gum or smoke. At sunset we all sat down to eat, and that was the schedule for the whole month. As time went on I noticed people weren't adhering as strongly as before.

There was a little village a few miles north of Tehran, very pretty, but it could get cold. Every summer my father would rent a truck. We put what we needed in the truck for three months, and went to the village to stay the summer. We camped on a private property in our tents. Usually we had more than one family with us so there were many of us together enjoying our vacation.

Life was so sweet and pleasant. A river wound through the village which was full of trout. In the evening all the fish were jumping. On both sides of the river were luscious cherry, apple, and nut trees. There was a little wooden bridge, a bakery, and a butcher shop with fresh meat. Everything was raised locally. If they needed meat they would slaughter a sheep and sell it fresh.

There was a pathway we walked down between the trees and a creek. The ground was rich with vegetation with which we made delicious soup. Everyone went to a cold water spring to drink. It was so nice and ice cold that you couldn't keep your hand in it for more than a minute.

Life was surreal. Everyone was more innocent and enjoyed uncomplicated things. Our whole family explored all around the area. A bunch of us kids swam in the river. We also caught fish. The girls cooked food and washed dishes, and the boys did heavier work.

One night we had a heavy downpour of rain and I saw people singing a song together about the rain. People were contented and happy. After three months though, it came time to go home, and then back to school.

During summertime, it seemed all of Tehran was evacuated, but I am exaggerating. Many people went to the north of Iran which is surrounded by the Caspian Sea. The other side of Iran is bordered by Russia. If I'm not mistaken, it's about four hours from Tehran to the sea. The road from Tehran to there is beautiful. There's a river on one side and mountains on the other. You had to pass through a dam with a lake and tunnels. It has graceful, curving roads through canyons.

As you got closer to the sea, the environment became greener and more lush. There are many wonderful coastal towns.

People were friendly and would rent rooms to travelers from Tehran. Crowds of tourists were everywhere.

Rice fields were a popular business. People would cook the delicious rice and kabobs and enjoy the cultural foods. The best caviar is produced and exported from the Caspian Sea. White fish is from there as well and very delicious. Iranians preferred the fish from the Persian Gulf because they are tastier.

A smaller town further up was very cold and had lots of snow. People would ski on weekends. Of course people love to eat and you could smell food everywhere. We loved visiting there too.

Because I loved northern Iran, I visited it most often. It was fascinating and there were many beautiful places like this surrounded by mountains, streams and lakes. People think Iran is only a desert, but it's not. The desert has its own beauty and character, but it's not all of Iran.

Eventually, we sold our house and moved to a different town. This new town was very quiet. It had a lot of virgin land surrounded by beautiful mountains. There weren't many people or cars, and no pollution. We could see the mountains clearly. If you wanted to go anywhere, it wouldn't take long because there was no traffic.

In those days boys and girls had separate schools. They would let the girls go home an hour before the boys so they wouldn't be bothered by them. The school made the boys keep our hair short for sanitary reasons. We all had to have #2 Buzz cuts. That was a bummer. We also had to wear a white plastic collar as part of the uniform to keep it clean.

My school was close to home so I just walked back and forth every day. Schools disciplined students very harshly. If you didn't study or did something wrong the teacher or principal would get a stick and hit you on the palm of your hand. Kids would cry and we were very scared of it. Even before my time they would punish kids on the bottom of their feet. It was called falak.

Fortunately, I didn't experience that part, but I did on the palm of my hand many times, and it was painful. That was normal for the education system; at least it seemed so to me. I had a teacher, a big guy who slapped me on the face once, which shocked me terribly. A few of the teachers were very mean and would punish us for the smallest thing.

No wonder I didn't want to go to school. Of course, I knew my parents had been disciplined this way in their schools too. It seemed acceptable to them. I felt it was so wrong. We looked forward to when school ended for the day and we were free. We could breath and didn't have to go back until the next day.

It was the opposite of now, especially in the United States, where students appear to have too much freedom. It seems like the teachers are afraid of the students. Students have the latest technological devices, opportunities, and educational facilities. They take it for granted because they've never known any other way. They don't even know what we had to go through or what happened to us.

We didn't have many toys. I collected a few boards, a hammer, and wheels to make a little wagon. My friend and I would push each other faster and faster down the street. It was homemade fun. What could be more creative than that?

I thank God because my parents were very kind and loved me so much. My father was a hard worker. They bought me nice clothes. My mom paid special attention to make sure I ate enough. Her cooking was always so delicious. Her favorite ingredient was love. She was affectionate and held me every day, kissed me and paid a lot of attention to me. I felt like she knew me really well and had good intuition about me. My mom would give her life for me if necessary. I was very close to my dad, but when I grew up we weren't as connected for reasons I don't know.

One day in school we had a math class and the teacher wasn't qualified to be a teacher because of his moral character. He asked me a question which I couldn't answer. He called me a name in front of the students and they all started laughing. I can't even say the word here it is so vile. I felt humiliated and very small. I didn't want to tell my parents.

Today, I have no malice in my heart toward him. I pray for him because I believe the reason he did this is because someone did it to him or even worse. He must have believed it was okay somehow. This man didn't know moral character and didn't know how bad he could hurt someone. I'm 60 years old and I can still feel the pain in my heart. I pray to God to forgive him. And this is a fact.

I have no problem with anyone in my past. Many came into my life and treated me wrong and damaged me badly financially and, yet I have no hatred in my heart for them because in the heart of God is mercy. Living in hate is a satanic act and I have no relationship with Satan. I won't pursue his temptations, so I choose to forgive and that is a heavenly feeling.

I was getting a little older and wanted to go see the beautiful rich people's area Uptown. I observed the great contrast between that place and where we lived. That made an impression on me.

In 1975, Tehran had changed a lot. Tourists were coming from everywhere. We had American radio stations and we had cassette tapes of all the popular songs. Any song in America was here also, the next day.

In 1976, Northern Tehran was quite different from the south downtown area. It was very European. We saw women going from the south to the north with a veil or head cover on, and then take them off in the north. Going back, they would put them back on. I felt it was forced and they didn't like it. I had a few friends I hung with every day and we wanted to go to northern Iran to enjoy ourselves. I didn't have much opportunity for a job or money so we mostly went to look.

Record shops had pictures of American and European musicians and at the same time miniskirts were all the rage. The tone of the movies changed too. I always wanted to be an actor, but I didn't know anyone. Men had long hair and beards, bell-bottoms and polyester shirts. You could hear the Bee Gees, Donna Summer, Pink Floyd, and more playing in many cars. Top-of-the-line cars were showing up all around.

There were poor people too especially in the southern downtown area. Remember, this is one of the highest oil production countries in the world, but there are still many poor people.

167

I decided my life would be better in the United States. It wasn't my motive to go there and get rich. It wasn't even on my mind. My problem was I wanted to associate with pretty women and most of the time I had much success.

Tehran is surrounded by mountains. My friends and I used to climb the mountain on Saturday nights and camp. There was a restaurant with traditional food up there. North of Tehran was a village. It was owned only by rich people. The Shah, the King of Iran, had a couple of palaces up there. It was a quiet area. On top you could see all of Tehran with its sparkling city lights.

I just wanted to go uptown and explore all of the time. The cars were even more luxurious than the downtown cars. There were a few very classy restaurants, but pricey. Teens were driving Mercedes, but I took the bus or taxi. The rich kids would go to Europe or America to be educated. During summertime, they would come to Iran for holidays. We had different nightclubs in Tehran. People went to dance, drink and have fun.

At that time I met a very pretty girl and we wanted to marry. We had a sweet, innocent love for each other and talked about the future. I asked my parents to go to her family with me and ask if they would consent to our marriage. I took them and my grandparents to her house, but because I had no job, they refused it. We couldn't see each other anymore. I didn't know what to do. I had no job, no direction, and no hope.

My mother wanted me to be a doctor. I went to the University of Iran, but after a short time I didn't want to be there. I wanted to leave the country. My Mom, like any other, wanted the best for me. Today, I understand she loved me way more than I loved her because now I have a daughter and I love my daughter so much too. I believe parents all feel this way, because we didn't physically come from our children, they came from us and that's a big difference. Parents deserve more respect and love from their children, but children are the ones who always receive more love.

Military Duty

In Iran we have mandatory military service. I was not doing anything anyway, except wasting time, and those two years were an obstacle I had to get over. I signed up. When the time came, they put us on a bus and took us to a small town close to the border of Afghanistan and Iran. There was nothing there. I had to stay four months doing training. It was very hot, always windy and just very bleak being there. I have to say, even though it was unpleasant, this adversity actually forced me to become a stronger person. On occasion we got together with soldiers from the same town. Most of us were very depressed. Some were married. The food was okay, but the discipline very harsh.

After four months they divided the soldiers and had us go to different parts of Iran. They sent me to Bandar Abbas by the Persian Gulf. When I got there I felt lost and I missed my family terribly. They took us to a military station where we waited to be sent to different locations. After a week or two I was transferred a few hours further to Bandar Lengeh which was not much better. It was even more desolate.

Our station was next to the water and we had to stand guard-shift with a gun. All we did was sleep and guard, sleep and guard, on, on, and on. After a while they transferred me to a third and smaller place. They put me in a van with a couple guys and took us a few hours away to Gavbandi in the middle of nowhere. I was wondering to myself, O, my God, why did they send us here? What am I going to do here?

I was transferred yet again, but there was no road, so they took me by scooter. It was getting worse. In this place there were about 30 small adobe houses, some chickens and a few goats. It was pretty, but boring. The name of this station was Koosh Kenar. They had donkeys inside the station which they used to fetch water with buckets at the well. They taught me this particular skill, and when I got the water and came back, I also had to strain the small worms from it.

Our icebox was run with kerosene. We put the water in there to chill and drink it. One person had to cook, especially if they were good at it. I always wanted to cook and be off of guard duty. It was scary out there. They'd wake me at 2:00 a.m. to guard and I literally just had to stand there with a gun for two hours.

I stayed a couple of months and then I decided to run away. I found someone to take me by scooter, but another soldier called the bigger station ahead of us and said that Mohammad had run away. The soldiers stopped us and took us to the station. I assumed it was to punish me, but they just asked why I ran away.

I said, "I don't want to be here."

The Captain of the station was nice and asked me, "Where did you want to be?"

I said, "Not here."

He said "Okay. Stay here, and I will transfer you back to Bandar Lengeh."

I thought that was great because by now I had seen the worst. At Bandar Lengeh they gave me a jeep to drive, but I still had to guard the station. I also started cooking and met a couple of super nice guys who became my friends. I was now more comfortable but had to stay there for some time.

My mom sent me a plane ticket to go home for a week. It was so hard to get even a one week vacation. When I went home it was like Paris. I saw modern life again with real refrigerators, tap water in real glasses, and good food, but soon I had to go back.

So I came back to my post and they told me about a station on an island which had a lot of wildlife called Faror Island. I agreed to go.

The island was incredibly beautiful. I was taken in a fisherman's boat. Half way across they started fishing so of course I also fished. Closer to the island I could see how pretty it was. I took my bag and got off the boat. There I was introduced to a nice guy who became my best friend. Later, though, he wanted to run away which he did, and I never saw him again.

Usually we didn't wear our uniforms because outsiders had no reason to go there. It was still a peaceful time. I would walk to the edge of a cliff where I could see the horizon. Sometimes the sky was filled with many clouds, sometimes just blue. There were a lot of fish in the Gulf and therefore, many fishermen in boats. We would ask for fish and they gave it to us for free. We had pretty good food supplied to us. And we had a radio with Arabic and Persian music.

I was coming up on 18 months of service when we learned of an uprising in Tehran. It was clear everyone wanted to leave. We were all in an emotional state of high alert.

They transferred us back to Bandar Lengeh. Even there people demonstrated against the Shah. I made some calls home. They said there was a revolution happening and that the Shah had left the country. The Ayatollah had come back from France to Iran. Everyone was on the street to welcome the Ayatollah, everyone. He allowed all the soldiers to go with an honorable discharge. I had been in for 20 months.

Home Again

I finally came home and could feel the revolution in the air. There were many explosions in different parts of Tehran. The war had started between Iraq and Iran and was getting worse. I didn't know what to do. Every day they paraded caskets of the dead Iranian soldiers down the street to make us feel even more afraid and morose. We couldn't have any lights on after dark, not even a match flame. An Iraqi plane may see it and bomb us. Every night we saw them bombing. So many people were dying. We had to have a password to get from one neighborhood to the next. They would ask us, "Who are you? What's the password? Who are your mom and dad?" I hated being there and wanted to leave the country.

I didn't have money and besides, the government decided to close the borders. No one could leave. But I knew one day I would. I had to think about what I could do to survive. What skills would I need? I had to learn something. Maybe I'd go to medical school, but there was no money to pay tuition. My next idea was maybe I could learn to cut hair temporarily. During this time, we sold our house and we moved to a beautiful condo in uptown Tehran. I went to barbershops and asked if I could work in exchange for some training. But because I was young, or for some other reason, no one would help.

I walked many hours from the north of Tehran to the southern neighborhoods. Finally, there was one shop where the owner said to me, "Of course!" That was the first positive response I'd had. I was elated. I could tell the owner was a good guy. God bless him. After a couple of days a homeless man came around and the owner challenged me to cut his hair. That was my start of cutting hair. The owner was giggling to himself, probably thinking I'd make a big mess, but after five minutes he became serious and said, "Mohammad, soon people will come here and wait in line for you. You are very talented!"

I was so excited it made me work even harder for him. He'd bring food and we became like family. I stayed almost a year learning more than the basics. I was using hand clippers which were very difficult.

Every morning I would get up early and take the bus to go open the shop. The owner left the shop for vacation once and trusted me to take care of the business. I was brave and acted very professionally. They thought I was good at it. I cut my family and friends hair for free.

The government still wouldn't let anyone leave the country. I was wondering where I was going with my life. After hoping and waiting for two years we finally heard news that if anyone wanted to leave the country, they could now go. I got my passport and started looking for a visa anywhere, but no country I tried would give it to me because I was young and had no money.

It was very difficult to get accepted. The United States had currently no embassy in Iran because the Iranians kept American hostages for too long. It created problems between America and Iran which wasn't the citizen's fault. We had nothing to do with it.

Someone said Argentina would give visas right away. I went to the embassy of Argentina and asked for a visa, which was ready the next day. I knew I was leaving now and was very excited. I told everyone. Even the shop customers knew.

The government allowed people to take only $500.00 with them. I bought my ticket. The night before I left, my mom was very sad. Many people came to visit me knowing I was leaving. The next day everyone followed me to the airport. There were at least 30 people. My mom packed two big suitcases full of clothes. I didn't even know where I was going and I had to carry these things with me. She also gave me half a kilo of caviar. I then said goodbye. She was crying.

At security they did a body search to make sure only $500.00 was on me, but I didn't have it anyway. I boarded the plane for the long flight. When it took off I suddenly felt very lonely. I was going to Argentina where they speak Spanish. I only knew Farsi, but I had no fear for some reason. The first stop was Spain. I met some Iranians and we had a beer together. It was time for the next flight so we said our goodbyes. As the plane took off I realized I had left my caviar on the counter at the bar. I was frustrated and disappointed.

Argentina

I took a bus into downtown Buenos Aires. I couldn't communicate with anyone. I was walking with two big suitcases trying to find a cheap hotel. Everything was so strange to me. I saw unique restaurants. Women's fashions were very different from Iran where Iranian women had to cover up. People were drinking here, but in Iran we couldn't.

I had to spend a night at the park, but the cops came and kicked us all out. That was pretty scary. I just started walking and browsing. Finally, I found a cheap hotel and had to pay nightly. I couldn't communicate with the front desk very well. They told me there was a lady from Iran and asked if I'd like to meet her. I needed information on where to go, what to say, and where to buy food. I met her and she told me about the city and taught me some Spanish. They had a community kitchen so she told me to go buy pots and pans and cook for myself. That was the cheapest way to eat. So I would spend a few dollars and could eat for a couple days.

I was getting to know the neighborhood and I saw a very classy salon. I walked in and asked if they needed help. I told them I could cut hair, but I didn't speak Spanish. The owner was very kind and decided to help me. He saw my work and taught me even more. I didn't want to get rich, but just spend some time there to get my visa and come to the United States. The salon had over 30 employees. I became friends with them all. Occasionally, we went for pizza, and wine, and chitchatted.

I decided to go to the United States embassy to get a visa. It was denied. I got very depressed again, but was determined and knew I would one day go to United States of America. I didn't want to go home so I had to stay in Argentina.

I started speaking very broken Spanish so I could at least be understood. They spoke slowly so I could learn. The owner taught me about hair color, dryers and woman's cuts. People liked me because I was enthusiastic and I liked them, so I had lots of friends.

I stayed about four months, but in order to renew my visa I had to leave the country again. A friend named Martha told me to go to Uruguay by boat for the weekend. When I came back, her friend would issue me a visa. Uruguay was a very pretty, small, ocean-side country with beautiful people having fun and enjoying life.

After a few days I came back to Buenos Aires to the shop. It seemed everyone was happy to see me again, even the owner. I was glad. We were all good friends and they were teaching me Spanish and offering me tastes of their cooking. Martha wanted to be close to me. She was a very nice lady. She invited me to her house and her family treated me well. I think they knew she had feelings for me, but I didn't want to stay there. I was determined to go to America.

I called my family from time to time. Everything was good. In those days there were demonstrations in Buenos Aires, so I knew they had problems there too. No violence, just all about politics.

I stayed about eight months in total, but knew if I didn't do something, I'd stay there forever. I finally decided to leave and somehow enter into America illegally. Even Mexico wouldn't give visas back then, because they knew they were just steps from the United States.

Guatemala to Mexico was easier so I went to their embassy and got the visa. Again I had to leave my newfound friends who had been so good to me. I bought a ticket and said my goodbyes. Martha cried and that was a bad feeling for me. I went to the airport and we took off for Guatemala.

When I got there I had very little money, but at least I could speak Spanish. I left material things in Argentina in order to travel light. I remember how brave I was or maybe brain-less. But because of this, I am here today to tell this story.

Guatemala

When we landed I went downtown, found a cheap hotel and spent the night. In the morning I went out and found some coyote-smugglers talking to people. It seemed almost everyone knew someone who could help me. I spoke with a guy who said he'd take me to Mexico and then to the U.S. I said I'd pay him when I got to Texas. The cost would be $2,000.00. It was 1982. They said they could get me to Laredo, Texas. I agreed.

The next day, the smuggler took me to a town on the border of Guatemala and Mexico. We parked and then we started walking into Mexico. There was a security helicopter flying above us so we had to hide under a tree. The coyotes took me to a nice house with a lot of pretty trees. They left me there for six to seven hours, but I did have food to eat. In the evening they came back and we started walking again. At a river there was a large inner tube connected to a rope and on the other side there were other coyotes ready to pull us over. I didn't care. What could I do at this point anyway? It was rough, but we made it. A car was waiting for us. We got in and drove off. I was afraid we'd get caught. We stopped a few times for food. I didn't know what to eat so I just ate what they did. They said if the police stop us, don't talk.

After driving many hours we were close to the Mexican-American border. We spent the night at another house. I thought, *Where am I? What am I doing?* I met more new people the next day. I didn't know their names nor did I care.

Now another river. I saw one of the guys go toward a tree. There was a rope connected to it which he started to pull. A small boat came up from under the water. They drained the water and we got in and paddled to the other side. They then pushed it back under the water ready for the next customer.

The United States

Now I had entered the United States illegally and I was worried. I figured they had higher technology here to find me. We walked, but weren't allowed to talk. We walked for 11 hours. I could see an airport's red blinking lights, but it seemed forever before we got there because it was dark. We had to go through a lot of brush and my body was full of thorns and scratches. I was dirty and felt disgusting.

Now we were on farmland. The sky was filled with stars and a bit of moonlight so it was not completely black. There were a few people in front of me. I heard dogs barking as we got closer. I was scared, hungry, thirsty and tired, but we had to keep going. I fell down once from fatigue. I had no idea how much longer it would take. We walked all night. I said to myself, *I will never do something like this again.* Daylight was coming and we could see better. There were cars on the road. They made me wait under a bridge. I heard a military jet take off. It made such a huge noise I started to panic. Obviously, we were close to an air force base.

In a couple hours, the coyote came to me and asked about the money. I said, "I told you when I get there I will pay you. I negotiated and said He made a gesture to kill me (slice my neck) if I didn't pay. I said, "I will. Please trust me."

Some Iranian guy was supposed to pick us up to take us there. We walked toward the town. I was thirsty and hungry again. We went to a market nearby where I spotted a soda machine and drank. I was aware that people may wonder why I was so dirty and might become suspicious. I met my Iranian contact and one of the coyotes got in the car too. We were driving again. I wondered how much longer it would be to Alvin.

After two hours we finally got there. The coyote and I went into my friend's condo. We sat and were offered food and drink. My friend gave me the money which I handed to the coyote. He looked happy and satisfied.

He said, "You guys are good people."

I responded, "Thank you for trusting me and helping me." He left on good terms, thank God!

My friend introduced me to a lot of Iranians. Now I didn't feel so alone anymore and I could converse. I still couldn't speak English. I'd have to start all over again learning another language. I stayed a month. I had to get something going, but I wasn't legal so I couldn't work. I moved to Houston and had more opportunity. I stayed with another friend, but soon had to leave. I wanted my own life. There was a club in the neighborhood that was very crowded every night. It had a valet run by Iranians. I talked to them and said that I was illegal, but needed a job. I also needed to repay the $2,000.00 to my friend. Thankfully, they gave me a job as a valet. I saved my money and got a cheap apartment in a rough neighborhood. I moved in with nothing; no furniture, pillows, bed, or fresh clothes. Nothing. But at least I had a kitchen and could cook.

In about a month I bought an old Datsun. I had the "luxury life." There was a hole under the gearshift where I could see the ground, but now I could travel around a little. I lived with very little money, hard work, and determination. A lot of Iranians were going to universities, but I didn't have that advantage. I didn't come here to get rich, just to change my life.

Six months later I met a nice woman named Susan. She was a very good person and helped me a lot. I want to say that even today, Susan, the mother of my child, is closer to me than my family or friends. She is a very beautiful, kind person. I have the highest respect for her. She's the only one in the world I trust with all my heart. I pray for her every day. I hope someday I can do something extraordinary for her. God bless her.

I told Susan about my life and she wanted to help. We were chumming around, having fun seeing things. I was 27 and she was about my age. The only hobby we had in Houston was fishing, so we would travel to Galveston, Port Arthur and a place called Toledo Bend. They were all beautiful areas. Sometimes we would camp and go night fishing. We had a wonderful time. Even though I had more money than in the past Susan deserved more than I could do for her. Money was still tight.

It was hard to communicate with her because I couldn't speak English, so she started to teach me. I asked her to be my wife.

We got married at the courthouse, but to be legal I had to leave the country again and come back legally.

We worked very hard and saved enough money to go to Canada together. I knew she truly loved me and would do anything for me. I loved her very much too. We went to the American immigration in Canada. Immigration asked us questions and gave us a visa to be legal in the USA. We went to Niagara Falls to visit and spend a couple nights. We had such a good time, but I knew we were coming back to work very hard again.

At the airport immigration, they took us to two separate rooms and interviewed us. They were trying to scare us and said she could stay, but I had to go back to Iran because supposedly we had married for a green card.

I said, "No, we really do love each other." They could tell we were honest and let us come back.

We got to Houston and now I was legal so I could do something more lucrative than my current job in valet parking. I decided to get a State of Texas barber's license. My friend took me to Austin, Texas. I used my hand clippers. The state board people were wondering how I cut with these things because they weren't generally used that much anymore. They were satisfied and gave me my license. I was so happy. Now I could find a better job. I still had to work as a valet for a while, though.

My car was junk and as I was sitting in the car one day, a cop came by who knew me from working at the club.

He jumped in my car and said, "Chase that car!"

But my car wasn't very powerful. They were getting away from us, but he knew I was doing my best. The next time I saw him he asked how my car was. We had a good laugh. After that night he became a friend.

It was time for a new car. I asked my brother-in-law to co-sign a loan as I had no credit. He did and I bought my first nice car, a Cutlass two door. I was okay with the payments and paid them steadily. Things were looking up.

One day I opened my mail and saw my green card. I was so thrilled to see my name on it, I finally had my green card. I could now live much better. I had more confidence. At last I was legal in United States and I had my barber's license.

Now I had a good feeling because I finally got what I had been looking for after all these years. Even though I had a license to work as a barber I didn't do so in Houston. Susan and I had decided to move to California. So with a minimum of belongings, we moved.

California

We started in the Cutlass toward California. I didn't know if the car would make it as it was at least a two-day drive, but we had no problems. In Canoga Park, California, I had a friend who allowed us to stay for a while at his place. We stayed a week. I was seeking a job and small apartment at the same time. Soon we moved into our own place.

We were both working to pay bills. I started working at a toyshop. There was a barber school fairly close to it. I enrolled in that school and because of my Texas license I only had to complete 400 hours to get my California license. I bought a bicycle and used it to go to school so Susan could use the car for work. I did my best in school and got my license.

While in school I quit the toyshop and started working for a local newspaper selling subscriptions. It paid better. I had to go nightly door-to-door. Many people shut the door on me and one guy showed me his gun and said not to go back there anymore. Another guy escorted me to the elevator with his rifle. Many were very kind though and invited me in.

Believe it or not, I became a successful salesman. I won the best salesman plaque award, and a free TV.

Finally, I started working as a barber. The barbershop belonged to an older gentleman who knew his profession well and was generous about teaching it to me. I learned most of my techniques from him. After a year of working, Susan got into a car accident and the car was totaled. A few hours after the accident, she told me she was pregnant. Thankfully, she and the baby were fine. We received money from the insurance. It wasn't a lot as the car was old.

I was now seeking a barbershop of my own and found a spot. I rented the place. I started with two chairs I'd purchased from a retired barber and made this station my own. You could tell it was homemade by me.

As I was preparing the new place, people would come in wanting cuts right away. Therefore, I had a feeling it would become a busy barbershop. When I told my boss that I had opened my own shop he wished me well. I will always be grateful for his kindness.

After a short time I became quite busy. We didn't have a lot of barbershops around and clients liked my work. Before I knew it, I had to hire a few people. We went from two stations to seven within a couple years. Business was real good and my income was stable so now I could buy things.

Susan and I moved to Simi Valley and rented a house. Soon it was time for our daughter to be born. When I was in the delivery room and saw my daughter's face I cried. It was the most amazing event of my life. Now I had a little family. We would go to church occasionally. I just wanted to worship God.

The shop was very busy and popular. The whole town knew my name. I decided to become a permanent U.S. citizen because I knew I wasn't going to Iran anymore. I studied for the exam, passed the test, and went to the ceremony. I was now a United States citizen. I had come such a long way to get here.

I started teaching barbering to Susan and sent her to school in Los Angeles. She became very good at it.

It had now been 16 years since I left Iran. So I decided to go visit my family. Once in Iran, at airport immigration, they took me to a room and asked me why I took so long to come back. I told them I had a family and a new lifestyle and I live in the U.S. now.

They were accepting of this, but said, "For every year you weren't here, we are keeping you an hour longer." It was a joke. They were very nice, shook my hand, and I left the airport.

My family had a big celebration. I could see the changes in everyone. We were all older now. During my visit I noticed that I had changed personally. I thought differently now. I didn't feel like a stranger exactly, but somehow I was.

After three weeks I returned to the United States. The neighborhood where my shop was had once been very nice. But now it was changing and becoming worse. It was harder to work with some of the clients. I wasn't comfortable.

At the same time my wife and I decided to divorce after 17 years of marriage. She left for Texas with my daughter. Now I was here by myself, living alone. It made me sad.

I was tired of the neighborhood and had more clients than I could handle. There weren't any barber schools in the valley, and I realized I could teach instead of cut hair. I felt this aspiration stronger every day. Many of my clients knew I was leaving them. I didn't know how much money I would need or what I was getting into, but this was my decision and I wanted to keep going to this new level of my career. My next step was to open my first school.

So now you know my story. Do believe it. Be baptized in the name of the Father, the Son, and the Holy Spirit and receive your salvation. Amen

I Cannot Forget The Night You Called Me
I said, "Why did you call me?"
You said, "Because I love you."
I said, "I love you too."
You said, "No, you don't. You don't even know
me. How could you say that you love me?"
I said, "You are my God."
You said, "Yes, I am. I created you. I created the
universe. I created everything. But you don't
know me and you don't love me."
I said, "Why do you keep saying that? Everyone
knows you."
You said, "Not everyone knows me."
I said, "I always mentioning your name."
You said, "Yes, but you still don't know me. I
want you to get to know me."
I said, "How ?"
You said, "Just follow me," and I did.
I said, "How far should I come with you?"
You said, "Keep walking," and I did. I suddenly
saw the cross!"
I said, "Cross?!!"
You said, "See, Mohammad? You didn't know
me. Yes, that's me. I am your God. I am

Jesus."

I said, "I am full of shame. I did wrong all my life. I broke all your commandments and now you tell me that you still love me?"

You said, "Yes, I always love you because I am love. Mohammad, you don't understand. I am holy. Sin is against my nature. I just cannot except sin. You must understand and be holy. Tell everyone that I love them and I am waiting for them to come to me."